# COMMITMENT:
# KEY TO CHRISTIAN
# MATURITY

**Susan Muto**

and

**Adrian van Kaam**

# EPIPHANY
ASSOCIATION

©2010 Epiphany Books

All rights reserved. No part of this book may be reproduced or transmitted in any form or by any means, electronic or mechanical, including photocopying, recording or by any information storage and retrieval system without permission in writing from the Publisher.

Library of Congress Catalogue Number: 2010922776
ISBN: 978-1-880982-45-7

Published by

Epiphany Association
820 Crane Avenue
Pittsburgh, PA 15216-3050

Printed and bound in the United States of America

# Books by Adrian van Kaam and Susan Muto

Aging Gracefully

Am I Living A Spiritual Life?

The Commandments:
    Ten Ways to a Happy Life and a Healthy Soul

Christian Articulation of the Mystery
    (Formation Theology Series, Volume Two)

Commitment: Key to Christian Maturity

Diving Guidance: Seeking to Find and Follow the Will of God

Dynamics of Spiritual Direction

The Emergent Self

Epiphany Manual on the Art and Discipline of
    Formation-in-Common

Formation Guide to Becoming Spiritually Mature

Formation of the Christian Heart
    (Formation Theology Series, Volume Three)

Foundations of Christian Formation
    (Formation Theology Series, Volume One)

Growing through the Stress of Ministry

Harnessing Stress: A Spiritual Quest

Healthy and Holy Under Stress: A Royal Road to Wise Living

Living Our Christian Faith and Formation Traditions
    (Formation Theology Series, Volume Four)

The Participant Self

The Power of Appreciation:
    A New Approach to Personal and Relational Healing

Practicing the Prayer of Presence

Rediscovering the Meaning of Our Christian Personhood

Songs for Every Season

Stress and the Search for Happiness:
    A New Challenge for Christian Spirituality

Tell Me Who I Am

# CONTENTS

**INTRODUCTION** .............................. 1

**PART ONE—LIVING COMMITMENT** .......... 3

   I.  CALL AND COMMITMENT .............. 5
        Commitment and Consecration .............. 6
        Risk of Commitment ...................... 6
        Commitment and Direction ................ 7
        Faith in Our Call to Commitment ............ 8
        Faith and Fidelity ........................ 9

  II.  LIVING COMMITMENTS FAITHFULLY ... 11
        Choosing Our Call ........................ 12
        Limits of Our Call ........................ 12
        Seduction ................................ 13
        Appeal .................................. 14

 III.  FROM COMMITMENT
       TO CONSECRATION ...................... 16
        Heeding the Divine Depth of Our Life Call .... 17
        Heeding the Messages of Divine Providence .... 18

**PART TWO—COMMITMENT AND THE
THREEFOLD PATH** ............................ 23

 IV.  OBEDIENT LIVING AS LAITY ............ 25
        A Path for All ............................ 26
        Obedience as Readiness .................... 27
        Obedience as Willingness .................. 28
        Obedience as Dialogical .................... 29

  V.  LIVING POVERTY AS LAITY ............. 31
        The Wise Use of Things .................... 32
        Poverty and Detachment .................... 34

|   |   |   |
|---|---|---|
| | Poverty: A Spiritual Treasure | 35 |
| | Conditions for Living Poverty Joyfully | 37 |
| | Jesus' Way of Poverty | 39 |
| | Poverty and Commitment | 40 |
| VI. | LIVING CHASTELY AS CHRISTIAN LAY PEOPLE | 42 |
| | Appreciative Aspect of Human Love | 43 |
| | Co-Formative Power of Chaste Love | 44 |
| | Obstacles to and Conditions for Chaste Loving | 45 |
| | Christian Counsel of Chaste Love | 46 |
| | Charitable Power of Chaste Love | 47 |
| | Loving as Jesus Did | 49 |
| VII. | HEALING POWER OF THE THREEFOLD PATH | 51 |
| | The Healing Power of Obedience | 51 |
| | The Healing Power of Poverty | 52 |
| | The Healing Power of Love | 55 |

## PART THREE—LOVE AND COMMITMENT ... 59

|   |   |   |
|---|---|---|
| VIII. | MARITAL LOVE | 61 |
| | Living Commitment as Married Couples | 63 |
| | In Praise of Everydayness and Intimacy in Marriage | 65 |
| IX. | ROMANTIC LOVE—PRELUDE TO COMMITTED LOVE | 71 |
| | Falling in Love | 72 |
| | Gift of Romantic Love | 73 |
| | Conditions for Committed Love | 74 |
| X. | DISPOSITIONS OF COMMITTED MARITAL LOVE | 80 |
| | The Limits of Romantic Love | 83 |

|      | Fallacies of Romantic Love | 85 |
|---|---|---|
|      | Integration of the Married Life | 87 |
| XI.  | MARITAL SEXUALITY AND SPIRITUALITY | 89 |
|      | Sexuality as Dissonant | 90 |
|      | Sexuality as Consonant | 94 |
| XII. | MATURING IN CHRISTIAN LOVE | 97 |
|      | Other-Centered Love | 98 |
|      | The Celibate Dimension of Mature Love | 99 |
|      | Witness to Divine Love | 100 |
|      | Other-Centered Love Exemplified | 101 |
| XIII.| LIVING A COMMITTED SINGLE LIFE IN THE WORLD | 103 |
|      | Single Life as Sign | 105 |
|      | Singleness and Spiritual Dedication | 106 |
|      | Questioning One's Calling | 107 |
|      | Place of Lay Associations | 108 |
|      | Place of Spiritual Friendship in Single Life | 108 |
|      | Integration of the Single Life | 111 |

**PART FOUR—LIVING COMMUNITY** ........... 113

|      |  |  |
|---|---|---|
| XIV. | LIVING COMMUNITY AS LAITY | 115 |
|      | Congeniality | 118 |
|      | Compatibility | 119 |
|      | Compassion | 120 |
|      | Courage | 121 |
|      | Competence | 122 |
| XV.  | FORMING COMMUNITY IN THE HOLY SPIRIT | 124 |
|      | Marks of a Christian Formation Community | 125 |
|      | Manifestations of Graced Community | 128 |

## PART FIVE—COMMITMENT AND HUMAN WORK .......................... 131

XVI. WORK CONSCIOUSNESS
IN CHRISTIAN LAITY ................... 133
Change in the Mode and Meaning of Labor .... 134
Work with Money To Make Money .......... 135

XVII. FAITH AND WORK IN
THE WESTERN WORLD .................. 138
Death and Idle Work for Earthly Profit ........ 139
Double Life of Worldly Work
and Heavenly Piety .................... 142
Repression of the Awareness of the Split ....... 142

XVIII. FUNCTIONALISM AND FORMATIVE
COMMITMENT .......................... 144
History of Service ......................... 145
Dominance of Functionalism ................ 146
The Art of Play .......................... 146
Effects of Functionalism on the
Threefold Path ........................ 147
Functionalism and Obedience .............. 147
Functionalism and Committed Love ........ 148
Functionalism and Poverty ................ 149

XIX. THE DELETERIOUS EFFECT OF
HOMOGENEITY ON LAY FORMATION ... 151
Homogeneity and Alienation from Spiritual
Experience ........................... 153
Homogeneity, Groupism and Self-Alienation .... 153

XX. SPECIALIZATION AS ERODING
SPIRITUAL UNFOLDING ................ 156
Reaction to Specialization ................... 158
Effects of Specialization
on the Threefold Path .................. 159

| | | |
|---|---|---|
| XXI. | CULTURAL OBSTACLES | |
| | TO COMMITMENT | 160 |
| | Rationalism | 160 |
| | Behaviorism | 161 |
| | Existentialism | 164 |
| | Pietism | 167 |
| XXII. | LAITY IN THE WORKPLACE | 169 |
| | Dedication in the Workplace | 170 |
| | Depletion Process in the Workplace | 171 |
| | Marks of a Christian Presence Crisis | 172 |
| | Negative and Positive Solutions | 173 |
| | Fostering Appreciation | 174 |
| | Conditions Reforming and Facilitating Christian Presence | 175 |
| |     Empathic Appreciation | 177 |
| |     Expressive Communication | 177 |
| |     Manifest Joyousness | 178 |
| | Repletion Sessions | 179 |

## PART SIX—COMMITMENT AND PRAYERFUL LIVING AS LAITY ............ 183

| | | |
|---|---|---|
| XXIII. | DAILY DEEPENING AND | |
| | SPIRITUAL FRIGIDITY | 185 |
| | Spiritual Frigidity | 185 |
| | Need for Formation Counseling | 187 |
| | Influence of Childhood | 187 |
| | Conditions for Overcoming Spiritual Frigidity | 188 |
| | Healing of Our Interiority | 190 |
| XXIV. | SPIRITUAL DISCIPLINES AS AVENUES TO | |
| | COMMITTED LIVING | 192 |
| | Spiritual Renewal | 192 |
| | Attitudes Fostering Receptivity to God's Word | 194 |
| | Cultural Obstacles to Formative Reading | 195 |

|  | Restoration of Reading | 197 |
|---|---|---|
|  | Reading and Meditation | 199 |
|  | Attitudes That Ready Us for a Wider Vision | 201 |
| XXV. | PRAYER LIFE OF THE LAITY | 205 |
|  | The Path of Prayer | 205 |
|  | Different Ways of Prayer | 206 |
|  | Prayer of Presence | 207 |
|  | Practicing Prayer | 208 |

**BIBLIOGRAPHY** .................................210

# *Acknowledgments*

It is our delight to acknowledge at the beginning of this book all those who facilitated its writing on the formation of the laity through commitment and consecration.

Our gratefulness goes out first of all to the corporation and board of directors and to all the members of the Epiphany Association, an ecumenical formation community for Christian laity we founded in Pittsburgh ten years ago. Its members genuinely aspire to be the kind of community described in many of the chapters of this book. Ideas and practices presented in the following pages have been tried and discussed by them and applied in their serious search for maturation in Christian family, social, and professional life.

We are grateful also to the faculty, staff, and students of the graduate Institute of Formative Spirituality at Duquesne University. We felt blessed and privileged when the administration of the university appointed us successively as the first two directors of this prestigious research and teaching facility during its first twenty-five years of existence, which we celebrated in 1988. The discipline of formative spirituality with its empirical servant science of formation was developed during these inaugural years of study and writing. It forms the theoretical background of this book.

During these years we also learned much from our interaction as graduate professors with our esteemed colleagues, loyal students, and many audiences. This more popular communication on commitment is in part the fruit of their animated questions and discussions. However, as its authors, we assume full responsibility for what is contained between these covers.

Finally, we are most grateful to Marilyn Russell, who carefully and patiently processed the manuscript, its bibliography, and its many revisions, to Cay Hamilton, friend and member of the Association who assisted her, to our families, and to all the members, friends and benefactors of Epiphany. To one and all we offer sincere thanks and prayers for our own and their continued quest for spiritual deepening and commitment to Christ.

# Introduction

How do I as parent, merchant, medical doctor, secretary, lawyer, teacher, accountant, cab driver, millworker, firefighter . . . secure the foundations of Christian maturity? How do I grow in the Spirit not outside but inside my secular activities? What are the means by which I, as a committed lay Christian, can practice spirituality as distinct, for example, from the ways in which word and sacrament may be heard and implemented in everyday life by priest, monk, hermit, nun, minister, or secular institute member? These are the questions of people in the world who want to grow in the spiritual life.

It would be wrong to propose as an answer to the universal call to holiness the development of an exclusive "lay spirituality," a term we prefer not to use in this book, as if one could align a "spirituality of the laity" with other special schools, such as the Benedictine, Franciscan, Ignatian, Carmelite, or Spiritan. Christian formation, reformation and transformation are operations of the same Spirit in all baptized persons. Our aim, therefore, is not to posit a "lay spirituality," but to respond to the request for spiritual guidance as personal, communal and sacramental. In doing so we hope to show that graced commitment as such is a key to Christian maturity.

We propose this book as a beginning chapter in what may prove to be *the* crucial story of the advancement of Christ's reign into the coming millennia of Christianity. The "flock" of Christ may always be "little," but the message we are called to carry forth is essential for humanity if we are to live in peace, respect all persons, and humbly admit that by our own power we can never save ourselves or remedy the ills of the world unleashed by sin and deformation. If there is one message to which Christians must adhere it is that of "amazing grace" without which none of us could discover the deepest meaning of who we are and where we are being led by the Spirit.

# Part One

# Living Commitment

## Chapter I

## Call and Commitment

We make commitments all the time, when we accept a new position, exchange marriage vows, enter the military, seminary, convent, or choose the single life in the world. The same happens when we join a political party, an association of laity, a parish council, a group of dedicated persons. What is commitment? Humans have an innate ability to commit themselves to a person, project, or community they want to love and serve. A permanent commitment is distinct from a passing promise. It binds us to the relationships, organizations, and tasks to which we pledge fidelity over a lifetime. In the ordinary world of children to raise, bills to pay, dates to keep, we are normally not aware of the underlying call to be committed to God, self and others. We take it for granted.

Immersed in the anonymity of daily cares, we forget the undercurrent of commitment that carries us. Yet presence to our families, parishes and professional positions, to any form of labor or leisure should be an expression of the call to live in faithfulness within the everyday world wherein we find ourselves. Fidelity to everydayness is the way in which we respond to the invitation to grow in commitment to the tasks to which Father, Son and Holy Spirit call us uniquely.

## Commitment and Consecration

Christian commitment is a consecration of secular life in and with Christ to the Father. As bread and wine are changed during the eucharistic celebration into the body and blood of Jesus, so is the bread of our daily responsibility and the wine of our suffering transformed by commitment. Our ordinary lives become an offering of sacrificial love to the Father in the spirit of Jesus.

At certain graced moments we may experience the depth dimension of our committed life. Then the smallest things become signals of the "More Than," enabling us to consecrate ourselves more explicitly to the Trinity. In the disciplines and demands of daily life, we become true disciples.

Awareness of our call to commitment is at once beckoning and threatening. It threatens us because we cannot control that to which we should be committed. We experience that we are searchers, pilgrims on the road like others before us. We know despite uncertainty that we are called to do something with our life. It must not be wasted. But what are we to do? Where are we to go?

We cannot fully know our call nor all that it entails. We may catch glimpses of this or that facet of our direction, but it takes time to see it clearly. When we do become aware of it, we are free to accept or reject what is asked of us. We cannot predict the way in which our call will be disclosed. It remains a mystery known only to the Trinity. Even when we come to know our call, its implications will still exceed our grasp. Like it or not, we are plunged into the unknown by the very call that beckons us to a journey of discovery.

## Risk of Commitment

The consequences of commitment reach beyond what we can foresee. This leap into the dark explains why Christians may hesitate before they commit themselves to marriage. They cannot make light of a life commitment. Theirs can be no temporary vow. Yet even with the best program of marriage preparation they cannot foresee all that may happen. Sickness, misunderstanding, difficult or handicapped children, monetary failures, deaths—one could go on, but the picture is clear. Commitment is a risk.

This example, taken from marriage, is true of any call to fidelity. If you commit yourself to lead boy scouts, you pledge to cope with tedious tasks that may arise, with human tensions that are unavoidable. We cannot reap the rewards of commitment without being willing to assume its mundane responsibilities.

In spite of uncertitude, the call to commitment continues to beckon us. It is inviting, appealing, intriguing. It is as if we realize that if we cannot commit our lives, we may peter out. We risk living a meaningless existence, scattered and inconsistent. We may become imprisoned in the passing whims of the age. Or we find ourselves absorbed in functions that have lost the spark, the poetry of human vitality. We plod along like robots without inspiration.

We know that we must commit our lives to what God wants for us, even though this "what" remains mysterious initially. Fear and fascination commingle in our hearts, for each call involves the whole of our baptized life as participating in the Trinity. Here we stand on sacred ground in awe, fascinated and fearful at the same time.

## *Commitment and Direction*

The Spirit beckons us to give form to life in a unique way. We are persons in God's eyes with definite services to perform. Each step along the way reveals something more about the mosaic of our life. We must not be afraid when moments of darkness come upon us. After the night emerges the dawn of a sudden gleaming. In its light we become aware that whatever has happened to us so far reveals in hindsight a hidden consistency. The direction of providence has been there all along. We have not been alone, as we might have thought. There is a thread of meaning, a mysterious direction, to the strange detours of our journey.

The Holy Spirit may grant us at privileged moments some disclosure of the pointing of providence. It is improbable that such clarity will last indefinitely. It comes and goes, shines and fades over a lifetime. Sometimes we see clearly the meaning of our calling. Mostly we cannot grasp how what happens to us relates to the sacred plan of the Trinity from birth to death and beyond. We must bow before the Mystery. We must live in the darkness of faith, in the puzzlement of not knowing while still proceeding on the path God has set for us with all its problems and possibilities.

The mystery of a life call can never be underestimated. It may only gain in clarity as years go by. So much has to be taken into account. There is no little red phone in a secret box to which we can go and talk directly to God. No divine voice booms back to our puzzled minds the message, "Hello, dear Christian, here is my will."

## Faith in Our Call to Commitment

In faith we believe that every event, from the birth of a child to the death of a parent, is meaningful. Every encounter, from a passing meeting with a friend to an exchange of marriage vows, gives form to our existence. Every experience, from dressing for work in the morning to writing a position paper, blends together harmoniously in the story of our life. If we were asked in advance how pieces of a puzzle fall together, who of us could answer? How immensely more limited is our advance understanding of the divine direction that unifies our journey.

The divine formation of each life is an enigma. We can

only rest in the faith that God is always calling. He ceases to whisper his direction through the filter of seemingly unrelated incidents, choices and events—the claptrap of daily life that constitutes the harassed existence of lay Christians in the world.

Faith in our call and its unfolding grants us the flexibility to respond to myriad demands and details without losing track of their deeper meaning. We live in the faith that daily happenings are occasions for disclosures of a mysterious invitation. We remain ready to behold events as pointers to a wider meaning. The Trinity as beckoning inspires us to overcome threats and fears. It calls us forth to paths not anticipated, to new ways that are in tune with what has gone before, with what is yet to come.

## *Faith and Fidelity*

Faith is an attitude of readiness to respond to the unexpected. It is a willingness to harmonize our response to fresh challenges with our formation up to now. Faith is a treasure rooted in our partnership in the Trinity.

Fidelity generates a sensitivity to any disclosure of life's design the Spirit may grant to us. For example, commitment to your spouse is an expression of your call to the married life with this unique person. Fidelity can only be maintained in the nitty-gritty of marriage if you live out your original "yes" in a flexible yet firm way. Making a faith journey together means that you and your spouse will change—in maturity, health, stamina, sentiments, looks, dreams, and demands. To remain faithful to one another, when both of you have changed so much since the time of your initial commitment, demands loving adaptation, honest communication, and lasting dedication, a firm yet flexible disposition of fidelity of heart and firmness of mind.

Faith in our life call and its consequent commitments, as flowing from baptism, grants us strength and serenity. We look less for special things to do or for exciting events to experience. We simply trust the calling Trinity in the everyday events that make up our life. We are at peace when we live in this surrendered way. We find joy because we believe fully that we are loved by God as we are and deeply cherished for every deed of fidelity the Divine enables us to do.

*Chapter II*

# Living Commitments Faithfully

Our baptismal call comes alive in a variety of minor and major calls disclosed to us from youth to old age. On a given day we may be engaged in responding to any number of customary or unforeseen events. All reveal something of the direction our life will take. They range from the obvious, like keeping our calendar straight, to the unpredictable, like coping with a sudden accident.

Beyond these transitory calls stands one that is lasting, one that will influence our life more or less continuously, albeit often in hidden ways. This is the mystery of our deepest life call. It is at the root of the various states of life, positions or relationships within which we have to express who we are, what we hope to become. Shall I marry or remain single? Choose a profession in the world or join a religious community or secular institute? As we move from adolescence to adulthood, we become more acutely aware that the call to commit our lives in one direction necessarily limits our availability to move in the opposite. This tension between what can be and what is should not surprise us. It is humanly impossible to become everything we could or would want to be.

## Choosing Our Call

Human availability is subtle and complex. It has to do with personality makeup (are we gregarious, lethargic, extroverted, introspective?); with life history (ethnic background, time of birth, place in society); with environment (impoverished, wealthy, educated, illiterate); with talents (mechanical, manual, intellectual, expressive); with deficiencies (sickness, mental slowness, poor circumstances).

For example, Albert Einstein, Martin Luther King, and Dorothy Day were persons whose life call made them available to humanity in generous and effective ways. The style and manner of their availability was as different as could be. One was a scientific genius, the second a social reformer, the third an advocate for the poor. These examples illustrate that every call, with its subsequent range of availability, implies a corresponding unavailability. Einstein was creative, but he was not and could not be another Vincent van Gogh. King championed civil rights, but he had no time for intense empirical research like B. F. Skinner. Day took care of the homeless, but she could not design housing projects like those Frank Lloyd Wright might have done.

## Limits of Our Call

Adolescence is a time when we begin to experiment with possible paths to maturity. Adventuresome as we may be, sooner or later we are compelled to limit our availability, especially in relation to the choice of a life state (married or single) and the choice of a profession. We can only be or do so much, though we might always like more.

Time and again we have to choose the direction of our lives in the light of our divine calling. Only when we take this higher dimension into account can we commit ourselves maturely to all we are meant to be. Saying yes to what is right and having the courage to say no to what is wrong for us is a risk worth taking. Though we strive to bring our daily commitments into consonance with our divine call, there are obstacles that block the way.

## Seduction

At times the temptation to be or do something unfaithful to our call can be very seductive. While the example of sexual seduction comes readily to mind, the obstacle described here is more subtle and pervasive. Any invitation that does not direct itself to our humanity in its fullness can seduce us away from our commitment. Passions, fantasies and popular pulsations cloud our freedom and obscure our sense of responsibility.

An organization such as an investment firm may set out to attract young professionals by depicting in vivid terms the incredible status which acceptance in the firm will guarantee. The promises that employers hold out may influence employees to join the firm for the wrong reasons. The 1987 film *Wall Street* is an example of how one man's greed seduces a young employee almost to the point of total corruption.

What accounts for this response to seduction? Not inspired commitment, to be sure, but fascination. One becomes "fastened," as it were, to the seducer's promised ends—no matter what the means to achieve them may be. One may seem almost hypnotized by the attractive possibility of fulfilling wants gnawing at one's inner life and freedom. The seducer promises a fast way to guarantee this gratification, but alas only with empty promises.

Seduction may be masked as a "call" to give one's whole life "forever" to an enterprise, a person, a cause not in tune with the divine direction of one's journey. In fact, seduction and subsequent fascination are in the end partial, periodical and mundane, to say nothing of destructive of personal integrity and true community.

Seduction is partial in that it does not direct itself to the spiritual depth of persons. It addresses only partial needs (to be rich and famous, to be "in" with the crowd), but these "perks" are painted as the whole picture. The charming seducer may exploit such needs with the best of intentions. After all, what he or she proposes is always interpreted as "for our good."

Seduction is periodical or time-bound in its effect. No lasting life direction can be maintained on the basis of fulfilling partial needs alone. Raw power and status, as history reveals, are here today, gone tomorrow. Financial gain is ephemeral. Neither can mere fascination with a charismatic figure satisfy the longing heart for a lifetime. Disillusionment, even among the closest cohorts, is bound to set in.

Seduction is and remains mundane in its basic orientation. It cannot be transcendent. The Spirit never speaks to isolated needs or fears. For this would be detrimental to wholeness and responsibility, to faith and reason. Growth in the life of the Spirit calls for the gradual purifying of unenlightened fascination. In a time of moral confusion like our own, such growth is essential.

If seduction is an obstacle to hearing and heeding our life call, what is a facilitating condition?

## Appeal

Seduction tends to operate on the social, vital and functional levels of our life. "Appeal" is an invitation that moves us as spirit as distinguished from seductions directed to drives, ambitions and popular sentiments only. Appeal touches the unique, relatively free Christ-form of our soul. It does not play on passions for pleasure, power and possession. Neither does an appeal attempt by clever arguments or charming mannerisms to convince us to move in self-centered directions. Rather it reminds us to take into account the distinctly human horizon of our choices and commitments. What is appealed to is that in us which is personal, free and responsible.

The intuition that we must commit our hearts to something beyond self-centered satisfaction cannot be awakened by means of propaganda, persuasion or enticement. Practical plans may prepare us for the event of an enlightening appeal—after all, we must know and respect our talents and limits—but the moment of insight into the divine direction of our baptized life implies and transcends logical considerations. No amount of reasoning can explain the mysterious assent we give to the Spirit's appeal to commit ourselves in a certain way. It is something we know we have to do. If we do not do it, we risk a life of unhappiness.

Sometimes a spiritual appeal may come to us when we witness another's commitment to a person, task, cause or movement that transcends status and monetary considerations. We are not seduced but attracted to the goodness of a committed spirit in whom we behold proof of our own possibility for commitment.

To be faithful to our commitments is to participate as Christians in the process of calling humanity back to its spiritual purpose. Along the way we learn what it means to be faithful to our own graced destiny.

## Chapter III

# From Commitment to Consecration

Through baptism and the sacramental life, Christ dwells in us as a consecrating presence. His Spirit sanctifies our commitments from the smallest to the greatest. The most mysterious, inner point of our being is the Christ-form from whence we steadily emerge in the image God had of us from all eternity. The Spirit of Jesus illumines all that we are and encounter. His grace enables us to consecrate our mind, heart and soul, our common and special modes of commitment, to his reign in the world. In and through Christ, life with its sufferings and joys becomes a kind of eucharist. His grace elevates the appeal of commitment to that of a call to consecration, to oneness with the transforming will of God.

Consecration grants human commitments a divinely inspired complement. It binds the finite to the infinite, the temporal to the eternal. It endows the secular with its sacred point of reference, encompassing and elevating human motives to the realm of graced aspirations and inspirations so subtle they often go unnoticed.

Consecration brings life choices to a high point of perfection. Marriage can be lived on the mundane level of vows made and broken, as if it were a temporary commitment maintained as long as it feels good. Marriage can also be lived as a sacred "permanent" bond, drawing a couple into consecration. Their relationship grows beyond romantic fascination or contractual engagement. It obtains its deepest meaning. Marriage vows then become a means of consecrating the spouses to each other in the Trinity, the source of their marital commitment from the beginning. Human life cannot hope to reach its fullness and splendor if we refuse to move with God's grace from commitment to consecration. Two dynamics facilitate this growth.

## *Heeding the Divine Depth of Our Life Call*

Our life call is far from a casual occurrence. It is the Spirit's way of beckoning us out of pride and confusion to a commitment to serve God and others in this world. Our life call is a mystery, the depth of which none of us can ever penetrate. Because it has to do with the direction of our existence as a whole, it surpasses each transient and particular situation in which we find ourselves. This basic direction is not charted by us alone nor can it be fully expressed at any period in our fleeting existence. Paradoxically, we search for the direction of our life while in some way it finds us. In faith we see that everything that occurs on our journey is an expression of our vocation, whether we are able to discern it or not.

Heeding the divine depth of our life direction demands openness to its past, present and future manifestations. The ambiguity we feel is due to the indefinite aspect of our call. Many events require appraisal. We do not know what the future holds for us, what the implications of our decisions will be nor how they will fit into what has gone on before.

The experience of not being totally in control can be unnerving. Yet our powers of management are necessarily limited, for we cannot organize what we do not know. Uncertainty can be paralyzing or inviting, depending on our faith. Not knowing can make us anxious and insecure or relaxed and confident. It depends on the level of our trust in God. We may try to escape dread by falsifying our call. Lacking trust, we determine to define every detail of our existence in advance. We cut out the possibility of surprise. We opt for the certitude of tight dominance rather than for the playfulness of trusting surrender to the adventure of life.

Grasping for total security leads to delusion, for none of us is ultimately in control of anything. To the degree that we try to fixate the future details of our life in an ordered file, we will be unfaithful to the surprises Providence holds in store for us. We risk losing flexibility and a sense of adventure. Life becomes cramped, dull, lacking creativity. The movements of the Spirit are encapsulated in the functional outline we substitute for life in its fullness.

The attempt to plot with mathematical precision the course of our existence may be related to the inclination to treat ourselves as manipulable objects, as numbers to be moved around at will. We neglect the deeper truth that to be human is also to be unpredictable to some degree.

Unfortunately, we are tempted to deal with others in the same fashion. Far from respecting their personal destiny, we define them as the objects of our designs. We try to make them over, not in God's image of who they are but in our own. As we can paralyze ourselves, so we can paralyze others by reducing them and their lives to a pre-set outline of do's and don'ts. We work to convince them that we know what their future should be. At times parents unwittingly play "God" for their offspring, making it impossible for their children to be faithful to their unique life call. Some never escape the patterns of deformation set in motion by overly dominating parents.

## Heeding the Messages of Divine Providence

The more our spiritual life progresses, the more we are able to behold life as a pattern of providential events. It is not a haphazard collection of accidental happenings. When we stand back and view our whole course at moments of recollection, we see that what is being woven by the Divine Hand is in dialogue with the gifts and goals evoked by our successive life situations.

God is a Master Weaver. All facets of commitment are threads in a tapestry, pointing to a pattern of meaning. Life is not as fragmented as it may seem to those lacking faith. Disappointments and failures as well as celebrations and successes are expressions of a divine epiphany. Each happening reaches beyond itself to a mystery of transforming love. In faith we believe that an eternal, loving Mystery guides the world. In hope we trust that goodness will prevail despite evil inclinations and destructive acts. In charity we perceive that nothing happens outside of the guidance of an ultimately loving Presence.

The fourteenth-century English mystic, Julian of Norwich, writes in her book *Showings* that "All shall be well." She proclaims in one pithy sentence her faith in the guiding hand of God. Julian believes that the power of love in a mysterious way shepherds the whole course of things and remains lastingly concerned for the welfare of humans. She is sure this revelation of wellness will prevail in the face of obstacles and temptations. Bouts of disbelief and doubt may at times plague the soul, but nothing can shake the belief that "All shall be well." Providence is not an indifferent force but a benevolent presence that treasures each person.

Romano Guardini says in one of his conferences that providence means that we see Someone behind everything that transpires on our formation journey. God sees us at all moments and knows what is best for us. He never wills that we suffer unbearably. He is always there with his grace to help us make the best of it. For, as scripture assures us, not a hair falls from our heads without that being known by the Father (cf Lk 12:22–31).

Because we are limited in our grasp of these mysteries, we

are inclined to impose limits on the power of the Divine. We may think that the immensity of the universe renders detailed attention impossible. But who are we to say such a thing? The sun shines on the vineyards and ripens the grapes as if the sun had nothing better to do. In a similar vein, God's love shines in every corner of the cosmos, on every created thing, and especially within the faithful human heart. Rather than toss and turn in an effort to bring our lives under perfect control, we ought to rest a moment and simply let God love us.

The more we believe that everything that happens to us has some significance beyond what we see at first glance, the better we may be able to cope with pain and suffering. We can bind our sad hearts to a saving Heart more magnanimous than our own. What appears to be a limit from one point of view can become an opening for meeting Divine Love in a surrendered way filled to the brim with expectation. This meeting is not an escape from reality but an attunement to the Formation Mystery in and behind all things.

Who better than Christ knew hardship and suffering? Yet he accepted the cup; he commended his dying spirit to the Father. Trusting that there was more to his death than met the eye, he rose on the third day and was transformed in risen glory. Confident in the work of the Spirit and bound to the living heart of Christ, we too can move from death to resurrection, from despair to hope. It is the purpose of creative Love to guide us from what is to what can be if we flow with God's mysterious providence in cosmos and humanity.

At gifted moments on our faith journey, we may find ourselves because of special needs drawn more deeply into the orbit of God's consonant care. Our longing can be acute in times of physical stress, emotional confusion, spiritual aridity. Weak bodies, anxious minds, doubting spirits are not obstacles to transcendence. They can be avenues if in our freedom we turn to God and rely on his generosity.

Jesus cannot compel this act of trust; it is ours to make in a free response to grace. Once done, it strengthens us to the point where we can find meaning even in suffering. This grace of trust in Eternal Love begins to be written, as it were, into the marrow of our bones. Nothing can diminish it nor can we deny it. We know God is there for us, no matter what. He hears the cry of the poor. He responds to our most pressing needs. Such faith quiets our fear-ridden self. It guides us toward a more peaceful and loving future.

The Holy Spirit, the mystery of the living God, thus addresses us at every moment. The Spirit invites our creative cooperation with his loving plan for humanity and world. The call to commitment and consecration beckons us to behold the sacred significance of every person, thing and event. We begin to see as an opportunity for growth what appeared as merely an obstacle.

Trust in the Spirit tells us that what is happening is not merely a crisis, a moment of suffering, a prolonged pain but also a new possibility. With the help of grace, we can advance beyond the harshness of reality to a wider vision. One secret of spiritual growth is that we act in consonance with and not against the wisdom of the Spirit. We find through trial and error, sin and forgiveness, setbacks and new starts, what our true vocation is.

All the forces that go into the forming of a life—beauty, joy, laughter; disruption, sorrow, sadness—are part of the pattern. Each thread has its purpose in the whole design. Each burden can be a blessing in disguise. The choice is ours: to treat crisis either as a time of closure because of fear or as a time of openness because of faith. The latter choice reverberates with the conviction that even suffering can be accepted with hope and courage, not bitterness and resentment. We can do something about it—even if this means only to receive it graciously and to treat ourselves and others compassionately.

Gentle surrender and the inner readiness to accept as providential what God sends us strengthens us to act in accordance with the limits imposed on us by reality. We do not lay back passively and complain that "bad things always happen to good people" or that there is "nothing we can do about fate." We do not fall into the trap of believing that life is a useless passion, or that God is a kind of sadistic force raining suffering upon the innocent. Such depreciative thoughts are banished by the act of abandonment. To face courageously the shadows of pain and fear, to know that there is light at the end of even the darkest tunnel, is a mark of Christian maturity.

Our joy increases when we trust the transforming mystery of grace. The results of abandonment may not be forthcoming instantly. Our pain may persist for a while, but in the process of turning to God, we discover deep within our hearts the gifts of courage and competence. We sense that we are becoming God's instruments. We begin to understand, if only through a glass darkly, what St. Paul meant when he said with awe-filled abandonment: ". . . the life I live now is not my own; Christ is living in me . . . I will not treat God's gracious gift as pointless" (Gal 2:20–21).

*Part Two*

*Commitment and the Threefold Path*

## Chapter IV

# Obedient Living as Laity

Baptism graces us with the call to transform our lives as laity in Christ. Eucharist raises this calling to the level of communion with the Trinity. Confirmation strengthens us through the power of the Holy Spirit to maintain our commitments, even in the face of adversity, to consecrate ourselves daily to God in family, church and society. Complementing these sacraments of initiation are the evangelical counsels of obedience, poverty, and chastity. These are Christ's own directives for a new creation, for a transformation of our heart into his heart and of our world into the house of God.

The way in which we, as committed Christians, express these directives concretely determines the depth of our spiritual life. The actual living of the counsels differs, of course, in keeping with the variety of commitments which we daily implement as laity in the world. However different these may be, the threefold path remains the underpinning for any Christian formation whatsoever. Each counsel has to be lived in congeniality with a person's life call and corresponding commitments. The counsels should also be expressed in ways that are compatible with circumstances in which men and women find themselves. Moreover, their expression should be compassionate with one's own and others' vulnerability. Finally, as Christians on the way to maturity, we should grow daily in the courage to be committed to the counsels as Christ was. We should competently implement them in changing and challenging situations.

If we seek real growth in Christ, we must accept that there is nothing optional about the counsels. They are essential conditions for deepening. They make it possible for us to be formed in the image of God to which Jesus invites his disciples. In a sense, by virtue of our commitment and consecration, we forsake the freedom to choose self as our life's center. We know that in the end only Christ-centeredness can foster true freedom. For this reason the evangelical counsels invite allegiance not only from members of religious congregations and secular institutes but from all believers. This path is given by Jesus and upheld by the Church as a universal path of holiness. The question is: How can committed Christians understand and live all three directives in the world in response to Christ's forming presence?

## *A Path for All*

The evangelical counsels are pointers to a threefold path leading Christians to respond more fully to the Divine Formation Mystery hidden in the everyday world of labor, love and leisure. The pathway of spiritual living differentiates itself in three approaches to the Mystery. Traditionally, these ways are designated as obedience, poverty and chastity to correspond to three manifestations of God's presence in creation, namely, events, things and people. These expressions of creation are interwoven in the fabric of formation of every human being.

As Christians, we should be open to these disclosures as links in the golden chain of obedience to Christ and his church within our families, professions and cultures. The threefold path guides and inspires us to radiate spiritual values and ethical modes of conduct in society. The counsels are much more than human suggestions to be taken up or left behind. They are given by Jesus as distinct directives for true discipleship.

## Obedience as Readiness

The word *obedience* derives from the Latin *ob* and *audire*, meaning in English "to listen to." Obedience in the widest sense entails the graced openness of people to the providential meaning of events in their life. This respectful listening safeguards and secures human formation as distinctively human.

Disobedience is the proud stance of people who isolate themselves willfully from the flow of divine disclosures in everydayness. They refuse to open themselves to the meaning and reality of natural events (earthquakes, floods, fires), to cultural events (plays, movies, literature, music, art), to dehumanizing trends (discrimination, social injustice, threats of nuclear annihilation, ecological indifference, homelessness) as these influence our human predicament. Disobedience causes people to wall themselves off from reality, to block the full ramifications of these happenings by resisting the directives they contain.

Obedience, by contrast, is dynamic, not flaccid, apathetic, or overly passive. It is our ability to listen to new levels of meaning in events that occur, no matter how challenging or painful they may be. Obedience is never closed or static. It is ever ongoing and expanding. It involves our life as a whole— all that we are at a certain moment of our personal history and all that we can become. Every past experience affects our powers of listening to present and future. The past expands our knowledge and refines our sensitivity to what is happening now. Hence our powers of obedience mature as we grow in commitment and meet the future with courage.

The receptivity associated with an obedient heart does not mean that we can be open to everything. Limits must be respected. In fact, to be open to everything would practically mean to be committed to nothing. Wise obedience calls for prudent options. During our formation journey many choices are placed before us. There are almost too many to deal with in modern life. If we try to be open to every option at the same time, we might easily become paralyzed by indecision.

The openness asked of us by Jesus is not merely a question of gathering information; it invites us also to develop a disposition of surrender to anything that manifests itself as a possible disclosure of the divine direction of our life. For example, a gifted musician like Beethoven, born with a refined ear for sound, not only had a technical capacity to compose but also a spiritual sensitivity to the sacred meaning of melody. An educator like Montessori was able not only to teach correctly but to awaken children creatively to their gifts and to the experience of the inviting Spirit within them.

Obedience implies readiness to surrender to any manifestation of the Spirit as speaking in scripture and tradition, in church authority and teaching, as well as in the events that comprise our personal history. The Spirit guides our discipleship in obedience to Christ's formative word addressing mind and heart. Memory, anticipation and imagination, enlightened by grace, become servant sources of formation—reminders of who we are and promises of who we shall become when we obey the Eternal Word and overcome the tendency to listen only to our own desires.

*Obedience as Willingness*

Obedient listening does not bypass our common humanity. It takes into account our feelings and intuitions, our expertise and learning, our scientific, practical and poetic dispositions, our sensate and rational capacities. All of our senses, skills and insights have to be placed in dialogue with the truths and teachings of our tradition so that the decisions we make will be most in keeping with God's direction for us.

Like Jesus, Mary and Joseph in Nazareth, so must we learn to be listeners over a lifetime to the forming presence of God. Our graced disposition to listen creatively as disciples should ready us to abandon ourselves to the Divine Word, also in times of transition when we are not sure where to go or what to do. Often we know only that a familiar life form has to be succeeded by a less familiar one if we intend to grow.

When the readiness to surrender diminishes because of fear or disobedience, people close up like scared turtles. They are afraid that being open may mean making wrong choices. Rather than take a risk, they settle into a complacency that colors their life in gray tones.

Christian obedience is courageous because it is a sharing in the obedience of Jesus to his Father's will. To this end he committed himself from birth to death, in private and public life. As son of a carpenter, as an eager student of the scriptures, as a lauded teacher, he withheld nothing. He gave his all in obedience to the will of the Father. Listening in faith calls for the willingness to say "Yes, Father" to what is divinely formative of our life and world.

## *Obedience as Dialogical*

As lay Christians, we are called to incarnate our love for God by means of personal and professional participation in culture and society. For lay Christians in the world, the will of the Trinity is not revealed only or exclusively in one's interiority. Neither is God's will to be found only in pious books or outlines of moral behavior. Rather God's will comes to us in the form of appeals, invitations and challenges, in concrete dialogue with the people and events that make up our day-to-day life.

The Spirit of Jesus speaks to us not only individually but also through our families and communities, through other believers and people of good will. Each has a unique contribution to make. All differ in character, temperament, education, expression and affinity; all share the call to be obedient.

Given the fact of human perspectivity, respectful dialogue is essential. We must listen together to the many manifestations of the Formation Mystery in the world, for Christ is present in each of us in a unique way. The Master of formation is not the exclusive partner of any one member of the Mystical Body. He is alive in all who share the commitment to be disciples. As we listen respectfully to one another, our obedience becomes less exclusive and more cooperative. We experience what it means to be partners in the mystery of redemption.

The church is like a master-listener. Under the guidance of the Holy Spirit, it binds together partial views in a unifying wisdom pertaining to the formation of Christian life as such. Listening to and with the church fosters in Christian laity a participation in the culture, guided by word and sacrament, scripture and tradition. Personal intimacy with Christ and the disclosure of divine directives in one another and in the church as master-listener constitute the essential components of obedience. To commit ourselves to a life of obedience may at times prove to be counter-cultural, but such is the risk we take when we pray with Jesus to the Father, "Not my will but yours be done" (cf Mt 26:42).

## Chapter V

## Living Poverty as Laity

Open to the Spirit, we enjoy and enrich the world. We behold people, events and things as manifestations of the Formation Mystery, as gifts to be celebrated, as beauties to be blessed. Each person we meet, each situation we encounter, each object we possess is appreciated as worthy of care and celebration. In the preceding chapter, we saw that obedient listening in the Spirit enhances our openness to the formative meaning of events that occur in our life, both planned and circumstantial. In this chapter, we shall describe poverty as a disposition of the heart that informs our approach to the natural and cultural things in and around us. In poverty of spirit, objects, talents, knowledge and sensitivities are appreciated as gifts from God, as means to discover anew the forming energies of the loving Trinity that traverse the universe. The Holy Spirit inspires the poor in spirit to treat not only their talents and education but also outer things as "traces" or manifestations of the Mystery.

Recall the glorious words of Francis of Assisi in his Canticle of Brother Sun:

> Most high, all-powerful, all good, Lord!
> All praise is yours, all glory, all honor
> And all blessing.
> . . . . . . . . . . . . . .

> All praise is yours, my Lord, through all that you have made,
> And first my lord Brother Sun,
> Who brings the day; and light you give to us through him.
> How beautiful is he, how radiant in all his splendor!
> Of you, Most High, he bears the likeness.

Francis praises moon and stars, wind and air, water and fire, and our mother, earth. He sees in creation reason to sing of God's goodness.

Each creature great and small receives its innermost meaning and potency in the Formative Word, the Second Person of the Trinity. In Christ, with him, through him everything comes to be. Without him was made nothing that has been made (cf Jn 1:3). His deeds, as Francis says, are wonderful. Not even death is excluded from his outpouring of praise, for death, too, becomes the saint's "sister."

Witness for a moment a sensitive potter who forms mere clay into a work of art. Visitors tell of a famous sculptor in Japan who caressed clay so reverently that it was as if he were in a shrine, not a simple shed. Under the touch of his finely tuned fingers, a delicate vase took form. He approached his work with awe. When finally the acceptable shape emerged, he detached it from the wheel. He looked back upon what he had made with love while admitting that not even the finest touch could capture the mystery embedded in mere clay. It was and remained hidden in the mind of God.

## *The Wise Use of Things*

Poverty can be defined as a wise and respectful use not only of talents but also of outside things that takes into account their innermost form and considers how their use will affect others. Poverty points also to the command to share what we have with the poor in a manner that remains responsive to the demands of social and economic justice. Nothing could be more important in the maturation of a Christian than to grow daily in appreciation of the gifts of culture and nature. What are the ways in which inner and outer things can be used most wisely? How ought they to be distributed and shared to promote the common good of humanity and world?

Unfortunately, we can become so caught up in using and possessing objects and talents that we end up abusing them and others around us. Selfishly caring for things, greedily collecting them, can preoccupy us to such an extent that we become possessed by our possessions. All higher modes of presence to things are paralyzed. We no longer behold them as gifts we do not deserve but as luxuries to feed our greed. In that case, the love of money or any other type of inner or outer possession becomes the root of evil and makes it all but impossible for us to be sensitive to the needs of others.

Consider, for example, a man who is incapable of seeing past the material meaning of his car. He polishes it, boasts too much about it, spends countless hours tending it, would rather be driving in it than spending time with his wife and children. This "thing" becomes his "idol." Indeed, as the Lord cautioned, it is perhaps more difficult for this man, "rich" in the worship of things, to enter heaven than for a camel to pass through the eye of a needle (cf Mt 19:24). Care for and enjoyment of possessions should be moderated by a recurrent movement to distance ourselves from them while tending to them. As scripture says: We must be in the world but not of the world (cf 1 Jn 4:4–6). Returning to the example of car ownership, maybe the driver mentioned a moment ago could become more focally aware of his passion by spending a day traveling by bus or by helping a neighbor with his repairs. After such experiences, he might be able to see his own car as a gift to be wisely used for transportation, not to be abused as a "golden calf."

## Poverty and Detachment

The disposition of poverty both in spirit and toward material things suggests practice of another rhythm in life, that of detachment and attachment. We move toward detachment whenever our concerns for material possessions threaten to take precedence over everything else of importance, including God. John of the Cross suggests that it matters little whether we are tied to things with a heavy chain or a thin thread. In both cases this bondage will prevent us from spiritually soaring free as did Francis of Assisi by praising divine bounty and recognizing in beholding it that we are only servants.

One isolated dimension of things, such as, for example, their monetary, pragmatic, or utilitarian aspect, begins to drain off the richness and depth of all other meanings. A kind of blindness creeps into our life when we forget from whence all things emerge and to whom they and we shall return.

Poverty of spirit is a crucial corrective to human pride and the related obstacles it breeds like avarice and gluttony. Detachment prevents us from being tied permanently to things, from being fixated on only the surface dimension of their significance. We have to develop the ability of joyful and relaxed restraint. We must affirm the horizon against which things arise in their ultimate meaning as gifts and as pointers to the "More Than." Then possession can foster our intimacy with the Trinity and help us to share responsibility for the spiritualization of humanity.

The person freed from possessiveness may find the Source of all things in a sunset, in the smile of a child, in a painting, in a sip of wine, a crust of bread, an evening of good company.

Everywhere in culture and nature the Formation Mystery is waiting to reveal itself to eyes and hearts no longer burdened by the need to possess things disrespectfully. How sad it is that we are inclined to forget our commission to shepherd the sacred dimension of reality and instead to see the glass of wine, the lovely face before us, the house in which we live as if it were ours and ours alone. Our inclination to diminish their giftedness prevents us from going beyond the shell of things into the Mystery they hide. By not practicing poverty of spirit, it is paradoxically we who become impoverished. By possessing things outside of God, it is we who become poor. How easily we throw away our inheritance, fall from our innermost commitments, obscure the message of matter in its openness to the Mystery. We are like prodigal sons and daughters who have abandoned our Father's house, who have forsaken our mission to confess its ubiquitous epiphany.

## *Poverty: A Spiritual Treasure*

To be mature is to be poor of spirit. Especially in times of loneliness and suffering, all of us experience the dire poverty of brief lives.

> Lord, what is man, that you notice him;
> the son of man, that you take thought of him?
> Man is like a breath;
> his days, like a passing shadow (Ps 144:3–4).

How fragile life is when we think about it! What are fifty years, eighty years, one hundred years compared to eternity? Only by admitting our innate poverty can we begin our journey toward Christian maturity, for only then can we awaken to the grace of transcendence. Knowing we are poor enables us to unite in spirit with all who share the basic poverty of being human, for none of us can claim ultimate ownership in this world. We are tenants of the Transcendent, living on time borrowed from a storehouse of divine generosity.

To admit our poverty is to acknowledge our utter dependency and vulnerability. No wonder we occasionally feel anxious, frightened, uncertain. To overcome such dread, we may be compelled to bolster our egos by acquiring far more than we need. One disillusioned millionaire is said to have asked, "How many yachts can I water-ski behind?" No matter how much we have now, it does not change the fact that some day we shall have nothing. Possessions amassed in plenty do not take away the pervasive certainty that we remain vulnerable and dependent on our Creator alone.

Poverty of spirit implies acknowledgment of our *vulnerability*. Vulnerability invites us to surrender to God's compassion. Because we see that people, rich or poor, are in the same predicament, we can understand their anxiety and insecurity. This empathic movement helps us to forgive the anxious, greedy ways in which so many reach out for power, status and possession to overcome the dread of their emptiness.

Our everyday life in familial, professional, and social circumstances is stamped with the mark of poverty. It shows up as much in ordinary moments as in ecstasy. Few of us make headlines. We live simple, hidden lives, encompassed by routine duties and a lot of drudgery. Even the most joyful times pass away. Yet this everydayness protects us from becoming proud or from expecting wealth or fame as such to make us happy. The poverty of our ordinary condition can open us to streams of truth hidden in the heart of God yet flowing out to his faithful ones. That is why Jesus said thanks to his Father for revealing such truths to the simple and unlearned, to mere children, while concealing them from the worldly wise and boastfully learned (cf Mk 10:13–16).

We may also feel poor in the face of our own uniqueness.

Each of us is called to a singular mission in life, no matter how small and insignificant it may appear in the eyes of others. Our deepest uniqueness makes us in some way incomparable to others. At times this can lead to feelings of profound loneliness, as if we are orphaned, abandoned by God in a vast, potentially uncaring universe, bound on a fast train to eternity. The painful poverty of being singular reminds us that we may be unable to become what we truly are, no matter how hard we try. This pain is deepened by the accompanying awareness that we can never know totally who we are. We are dependent in some way on the successive happenings in our lives to disclose our calling. What we are describing here could be identified as the poverty of unpredictability.

The pathos of poverty is the beginning of maturity. To acknowledge our poverty is at the same time to reclaim our spiritual richness, for poverty is a symbolic pointer to our hunger and thirst for presence to the Most High.

## *Conditions for Living Poverty Joyfully*

The Christian transformation of poverty into spiritual wealth begins with detachment. To grow as followers of Jesus, we must detach ourselves from the surface meanings of creatures. Letting go of inordinate attachments frees us to see things reverently, in compatibility with their deepest form and meaning. Detachment from preoccupation with our own needs for security also enables us to hear the cry for justice, peace and mercy resounding throughout the earth. By the same token, detachment creates room for disclosures of the Divine Mystery in the midst of everydayness.

Daily distancing, or what the spiritual masters call "daily dying," frees our vision for the perception of ever deeper layers of meaning to be realized in our transformation of the world as Christian laity. This graced vision enables us to form culture and nature in consonance with the divine destiny of human history.

Another condition for living poverty joyfully is hope. We can never live at ease with our poverty without access to the divine gift of hope. Hope, even in the midst of apparent hopelessness, points us toward the More Than, toward the Eschaton, toward our full transformation in the Risen Lord. In spiritual and material poverty, he is there beckoning us to remain hopeful, to enjoy the truth that we are already, since baptism, on the road toward paradise. In spite of our failures, we are filled with hope in the promise of future transformation still hidden from our sight.

Hope teaches us that what this world can offer is not lasting peace. Nothing but God can fulfill the restless yearning of our heart. If hope dies or loses its orientation to eternity, we may be tempted to replace the Eschaton of revelation by an "eschaton" of our own technical or temporal illusions. We may be seduced by the idle expectation of creating a niche of history that will satisfy all dreams of humanity. This false hope has to die because it makes us cling to things inside ourselves (images and ideas) and outside ourselves (possessions) as if they were "gods."

In the light of hope, we are slowly loosened from the things on which our hopes may be glued. Hope is a lasting disposition of the heart. It enables us to deal with things in a caring yet detached manner, as stewards not owners. We can rejoice in them insofar as they help to create passing moments, periods or eras of peace and justice. These creations of ours then become pointers to the ultimate glorious form of redeemed humanity. They foreshadow the house of God to come. They help to weave the golden thread of hope through the history of humanity, for, since the Fall, we perch always on the edge of despair. What keeps hope alive generation after generation is this chain of symbolic pointers. The limited goodness, truth and loveliness of the things of this world can be enjoyed and praised in thanksgiving as a disclosure of the world awaiting us in times to come.

## Jesus' Way of Poverty

The Lord of formation himself was filled with tender respect for creation. His sensitivity vibrates in his words as when he speaks in parables about lilies of the field and little sparrows cared for so gently by him that not one falls without his knowing it (cf Mt 6:26–34). Jesus asks us in the midst of our poverty to place our trust in the Father, not to give in to despair. He tells us that the Father's love will never be taken away from us. He shows us in countless ways how the gifts of nature and culture should be used respectfully and lovingly in inner detachment and poverty of spirit.

Visiting a wedding party, Jesus makes available in a wondrous way the finest wine so that the guests may have a delightful time (cf Jn 2:1–11). He multiplies loaves and fishes so that the crowd following him can still their hunger and regain strength (cf Mk 6:34–44; 8:1–9). When his apostles are not able to catch fish, Jesus instructs them to set their nets again into the water where they are filled to the breaking point (cf Lk 5:1–11). When Mary in a beautiful gesture of respectful presence pours fragrant and expensive oil over his feet, he blesses her and tells the murmuring guests that she did the right thing. He reprimands them when they complain that this precious oil should have been sold and the money given to the poor (cf Jn 12:1–8). Their complaint reflects a one-sided materialistic view of poverty. Their indignation betrays the compassion we should show also for those who are aesthetically and symbolically poor. For their sake we should adorn the world so that all may celebrate it as the house of God.

This respectful attitude toward the gifts of culture and

nature became such a hallmark of Jesus' life that one of the main attacks on him was that he was a drinker of wine, a man without asceticism, who allowed his disciples to eat the corn of the fields on the sabbath (cf Mt 12:1–8). Jesus' relaxed presence to the gifts of the Father was only possible because of his ability to distance himself from the mere material meaning of things and to reveal a higher message. He said: "It is mercy I desire and not sacrifice" (Mt 12:7). Jesus never became enslaved to things but strove always to discover and celebrate their hidden potential in accordance with providential life situations and the demands of justice, peace and mercy.

Poverty thus gives rise to the celebration of creation. Jesus was so freed from things that he could honestly say he did not possess a stone on which to lay his head (cf Lk 9:58). This does not mean that he never found a place to sleep, for he often stayed in the homes of friends like Martha and Mary. It only emphasizes that he kept himself free from absorption in such concerns. To follow his example does not mean forsaking in a quietistic fashion interests in food, shelter, clothing, knowledge, beauty; it means only that we trust God enough not to be absorbed by such preoccupations.

## *Poverty and Commitment*

A basic condition for the practice of poverty is and remains respect for the singular uniqueness of each person in regard to his or her life call, physical health, sensibility, insight, background and responsibility. A sign of mature Christian commitment is the readiness to take these factors into account in our dealings with people, for only in this way can we avoid being too judgmental. What is the wise and respectful use of things for one person may prove to be unwise and disrespectful for another. In short, there is infinite variety in the individual practice of poverty. It varies from one person to another. It can also be different in different periods of our life, for as we change and grow so must the practice of poverty alter accordingly.

Uppermost in this kind of maturing is not the practice itself but the spirit of Christ in which our poverty is lived. Therefore, the practice of poverty should never become fanatical, rigid, inflexible or isolated from our special commitments in Christ. It should be open to change in our life and in the situation in which we are called to use things in the best interest of our own and others' rights and needs.

For this reason Christians must become increasingly sensitive to people who are spiritually and physically poor and abandoned. The attitude of Christ, which must become our own, is his kenotic love, his willingness to empty himself, not to cling to anything, not even his equality with God. Instead he chose to become a servant, a choice that enabled him also to be uniquely effective for ages hence (cf Phil 2:1–11). Jesus shows us, as does his mother Mary, that God, who is mighty, does great things through those who become instruments in his hands. The Holy Spirit wants to transform us into ever more refined channels through which God's work of transforming the world can be brought to fruition (cf Lk 1:46–55).

## Chapter VI

## Living Chastely as Christian Lay People

Our formation in the world never occurs in isolation but always in interwovenness with events and things. Most of all, it unfolds in relation to people whom we encounter intimately or casually in daily life. Undoubtedly, of these three disclosures of God's love, the human person is the highest. To understand people in their agony and ecstasy, their smallness and greatness, their hiddenness and notoriety, we need to let go of our own agendas, to pay loving attention to them, feel at one with them, care for them in true appreciation. Such is the Great Commandment. We are to love God first and, secondly, to love others as we love ourselves (cf Mt 22:34-39). For Christians the love of self and neighbor is an expression of the divine gift of charity. This gift enables us to stretch our hearts and hands toward others, to see them as epiphanies of the Formation Mystery.

We humans can choose to love or hate, to be kind or mean, indifferent or compassionate. We have the freedom to destroy or create, to put down or raise up, to reduce or elevate others. In our selfishness and sinfulness, we can suppress loving dispositions and close our hearts to grace. The latter choice is disastrous. Without love it is impossible to enjoy a truly human and spiritual life.

## Appreciative Aspect of Human Love

Our lives from their earliest days are an invitation to togetherness. This beckoning follows us from birth to death. It is connected with the transcendent openness we are as graced human beings. Love is more than fuzzy feelings. Mature love expresses itself in sensitive and responsible thoughts, acts, affects and commitments.

Husband and wife must refine their understanding of each other's uniqueness. They must create space for one another to unfold. Otherwise they risk violating each other's integrity. Unenlightened love hampers rather than helps the other to grow; it smothers rather than frees.

In regard to ourselves, lack of loving respect has a similar effect. It may lead to violence against ourselves. This usually takes the form of a misguided appraisal of who we are. Such misunderstanding makes us strive to become what we cannot be. It is as if an artist were to compel himself to be an auto mechanic or a born farmer or librarian. In this case lack of appreciation of our call and its commitments may lead to spiritual self-abuse. We abuse our calling either by refusal to listen to its inspiration or by falsifying its expression in uncongenial commitments.

To cite another example, a person may be called to compose classical music. However, the composition of more vulgar melodies pays well and promises more popularity. Hence he or she may resist being faithful to the "still small voice within." The same would be true of a born popular singer who invests all her energy in futile attempts to be a classical composer.

Expressing the appreciative aspect of human love is the phrase "chaste love." It would be unwise to limit this expression only to a concern for genital sexual behavior or only for those moral principles that govern pre-marital and marital sexuality. "Chaste love" is too rich a concept for us to believe that our love is acceptable in the eyes of God so long as we do not abuse another bodily. Chaste or appreciative love is more comprehensive than the mere avoidance of physical violence or sexual harassment. To learn to live chastely and lovingly in the spirit of Christ takes a lifetime. The disposition of commitment to a loving presence to self and others, in or outside of marriage, has to grow throughout our adult life. Mature love in no way violates others' integrity, ravishes their dignity, suppresses their right to privacy, or blocks their unique unfolding.

## Co-Formative Power of Chaste Love

The commitment to chastity or to non-violation of the integrity of self and others is a fundamental ingredient of human love. Its absence or pretense can be terribly destructive. Many novels deal with this theme in a manner that is timeless. To name a few: D. H. Lawrence's *Fathers and Sons;* Henry James' *Portrait of a Lady;* William Golding's *Lord of the Flies.* Conversely, appreciative love, chaste, mature and committed, grants us the greatest power for self-formation and the formation of others. The love Anne Frank reveals in her *Diary of a Young Girl* is an example. Anne's words invite us to lower our defenses and to trust the basic possibilities for goodness in others even under the most adverse conditions. Love like this is freeing, humanizing. It grants us the power to bring into the light of day our strengths and weaknesses, our joys and sorrows, our hopes and failures.

At its height chaste love enables us to commit ourselves to a beloved human person, to experience the co-formation loving commitment makes possible. Take the oft repeated story of a spouse who remains faithful to a husband or wife who is suffering from an incurable disease or paralyzed after an accident. No one can explain, humanly speaking, such impeccable commitment. Indeed we see in relationships like these something of the pure mercy and generous love of Jesus himself.

## Obstacles to and Conditions for Chaste Loving

Unfortunately, the masks love wears are not all chaste. Love can be based on pretense. Often violence masquerades as loving commitment, opening its victims to abuse. One thinks of parents, friends or relatives who arbitrarily impose their will on hapless children—an imposition tragically portrayed in Ingmar Bergman's film, *Fanny and Alexander*. Many children's lives lose their graced course because of the way in which elders impose their own dreams and desires on a child, albeit in tones of sweet concern.

The awareness of this threat to our integrity may alert us to the necessity of chastity in both an intellectual and an emotional sense. Not only must we avoid "raping" another psychologically; we must strive continually to replace violent forms of love with the disposition of sincere commitment to the dignity and goodness of the other. The condition for the possibility of chastening our love and for recovering respectful communion is the overcoming of needy, imposing, begging and overwhelming forms of violent or seductive love versus virtuous love.

In our growth toward human and spiritual maturity, love is inevitably mixed with self-centered drives and compulsions. We carry with us, for a long time, these immature tendencies. Instead of being appreciative and committed, love becomes depreciative and uncommitted.

As infants and small children, we are dependent on our parents for sustenance. We cannot yet temper our demands on their attention. Our needs are simply too great. Only over time can we grow to a way of loving that transcends the fulfillment of our need to get what we want when and how we want it.

In other words, to become fully human and truly committed, love has to be "chastened" or "purified" of self-centered passions and purposes, anxious needs and overdependent demands. Only when love is chaste can we diminish the tendency to use and abuse ourselves and others as commodities for pleasure, as sources of need fulfillment or ego-enhancement.

## Christian Counsel of Chaste Love

While obedience enhances our ability to listen to the divine directives in events, while poverty of spirit reminds us of our dependence on God, committed love makes us friends and companions with one another on the road of maturation in the Lord. Clearly, disobedience and arrogant self-sufficiency are forces that promote closure to the directives of God's providence; they alienate us from the divine formation power guiding daily events in a meaningful way. Lack of mature love is another major source of dissonance. It separates us in particular from God's own love as reflected in the unique images of God that people are called to be.

The counsel of chaste love has been given to us by Jesus himself.

> This is my commandment:
> love one another
> as I have loved you.
> There is no greater love than this:
> to lay down one's life for one's friends.
> You are my friends
> if you do what I command you.
> . . . . . . . . . . . . . . . .
> The command I give you is this,
> that you love one another (Jn 15:13–17).

In and through this counsel, we are invited by Jesus to love ourselves in congeniality with our divine call and compatibility with others. If we fail to appreciate our own call, how can we expect to love that same calling in our neighbor? How can we expect to be committed to it?

A decrease in faithfulness to this counsel diminishes the possibility of integration of our life as well as a sense of compatible involvement in society. The counsel of chaste love empowers us beyond anything else to accept ourselves wholeheartedly as emerging from the Divine Formation Mystery in dialogue with our ever evolving life situations.

Paradoxically, the height of this counsel to self-appreciation and commitment implies the depth of humility. To walk in the truth of who we are is to be humble. Humility does not cancel appreciation of our gifts. Therefore, the most profound act of humility is to acknowledge and affirm the limited yet loving persons we are called to become.

## Charitable Power of Chaste Love

The charitable power of Christian love should not be understood in a narrow way. Its thrust is inclusive. Small-mindedness would restrict such freeing love to its most ostentatious expressions, such as the immediate relief of certain needs for physical nurturing, clothing or shelter. Essential as such expressions of love are, the counsel of Jesus to love extends beyond these acts of good will to other, perhaps less noticeable, incarnations of love that may be of benefit to many.

For example, we may be inspired, together with colleagues who went before us and will go after us, to incarnate Jesus' love for humanity and its formation by commitment to scholarship, artistic creation, or scientific research. Some scientists, for example, may accomplish much for humanity by their endeavors. They provide for the common good as do others who spend their time and generosity as social workers feeding the hungry and sheltering the homeless. By means of study and research, their scientific labors may hasten the moment in which a new insight of benefit to sick or starving populations may be born. If our love for humanity is chaste, and hence not exclusively profit- or reward-oriented, it may lead to the birth of new knowledge that will benefit not only one group in need but thousands. Such would be the work of a Louis Pasteur or a Jonas Salk. Untold millions have profited from their love for humanity expressed in tedious hours of laboratory experimentation.

Possibly a certain technical, economic or scientific development, born out of loving commitment to humanity, may remove the very causes of poverty plaguing an entire population. Researches in agriculture, medicine and marine biology are notable in this regard. Likewise, it may also be that the emergence of a new form of artistic expression, out of love for beauty, may bring untold millions to renewed appreciation of the Sacred in culture and nature.

We may dread the thought of embodying our Christian love in the service of humanity by commitment to study, research, or artistic production. But where would the world be without the efforts of an Albert Einstein or a Vincent van Gogh? Where would their work have been without their unnamed predecessors, assistants, or patrons? For us, too, there may be no immediate rewards for years of loyal service, no warm sympathy, no admiring headlines. We may be tempted to give up when we do not experience the here and now effectiveness of our loving endeavors. We may die long before anyone acknowledges the enterprises to which we have given ourselves. We may never witness the victory over human needs to which we have dedicated our lives. Yet in some way we know that this victory may only come about because innumerable loving people spent time and effort in dedicated study to serve the common good.

### Loving as Jesus Did

The counsel of Jesus to chasten our love by loving one another as he has loved us may mean that people in the world are called to be for the most part hidden servants, quiet lovers, silent witnesses. Our love for Christ should free us to pursue this way of committed love in spite of anonymity and its sometimes exhausting, often unrewarded responsibilities.

The awareness that the Word was made flesh and dwells among us, full of grace and truth, full of love, gives a whole new, unsuspected divine dimension to the Christian's call to love self, others and God. Jesus told us as well that whatever we do to the least appreciated persons on earth we do to him. He described how at the end of time people will ask him in surprise when they clothed him or gave him a drink or visited him in prison. And the Lord will reply that whenever they did so to the least of their brothers and sisters, they did so to him (cf Mt 25:31–46).

Christian professionals who are called to serve the suffering Christ in humanity in the anonymity of seemingly endless labors in study halls, operating rooms, consultation offices and laboratories can serve the Lord in whatever they do if they do so out of love for others and in the name of the Lord. The same applies to Christian electricians, fire fighters, street cleaners, factory workers, cab drivers, secretaries, housekeepers, and so on. All who give in love receive love from and give love in turn to the Lord.

Chaste Christian love is thus an ongoing challenge, implying both divine appreciation and human cooperation. We must continually strive to affirm ourselves and confirm others because of the transforming love of Christ for each of us. All are loved by him, and hence all are worthy of our love. The coming of the Light into the world in the person of Christ makes possible and infinitely promotes our emergence from the lackluster conviviality of crowd and collectivity to the Christ-like committed love of communion and community.

## Chapter VII

# Healing Power of the Threefold Path

The dividing forces of civilization seem to be stronger than those of integration. We need to be made whole, to be healed. Healing restores to wholeness what is wounded or disrupted. The need for healing is obvious when we are ill. Physicians are persons trained to restore our injured bodies to wholeness. They work with nature to reintegrate a diseased organism within the harmonious functioning of the body as a whole. Healing, or making whole, is also necessary for our personality. An absence of harmony in our life may lead to diseases that mar effectiveness. They diminish the ability to function well.

We should be committed to the formation of a healing disposition. The road to such wholeness and harmony can be found in the threefold path laity are called to live in their own fashion.

### *The Healing Power of Obedience*

As we have seen, obedience is the willingness to listen to reality. Everyday reality can be seen as a disclosure of possibilities to be given form to in our here and now situation. By contrast disobedience is our unwillingness to listen to life unless it serves selfish aims. Disobedience is a divisive force. It is the mother of isolation, fragmentation and closure.

Obedience is an integrating, connecting attitude. Disobedience, as a source of isolation, separates us from the Formation Mystery as embracing all of humanity and history. It isolates us from other people, from cosmos, nature and society and from their transcendent meaning.

Disobedience is a principle of fragmentation. It blocks our openness to reality. It filters our perception, telling us what we shall and shall not experience. Life becomes more and more compartmentalized. To be "successfully disobedient," we must develop and maintain an armory of defensive tactics, preventing us from becoming aware of anything that might throw into question our present perceptions. Tension may be evidenced by psychosomatic symptoms or neurotic reactions. It is felt acutely when anything threatens to break through the wall of our resistance to reality. As a force of closure, disobedience is the refusal to be receptive to any new insight that may conflict with the comfortable or complacent style to which we cling in the present.

People are inclined to organize their life around self-centered concerns that leave little room for the disclosure of transcendent directives. These are often dismissed as distractions which limit fun or productivity. Functional production to the exclusion of commitment to what we are called to be is a sign of disobedience. Refusal to allow the mystery of God's love to reveal itself in human life and society halts spiritual maturation. It erodes Christian commitment. Obedience is one power that can heal fragmentation and restore our oneness with a redeemed and transfigured cosmos.

## *The Healing Power of Poverty*

Our attitude toward things is divisive when we perceive them for their own sake, when we exclude any reference to their divine source or use them merely for selfish gain. Fascination with matter and its possession makes it difficult for us to sense the spiritual horizon of our world. Our estimation of what is most valuable narrows to the point where we see things merely as materials to be owned or collected.

Besides distorting our appreciation of things in God, a merely possessive view of their meaning obscures other aspirations of the heart. We silence these outcries of our deepest being for more than mere possessiveness. We cling anxiously to wealth and security. We become unable to see ourselves as epiphanic persons because we cannot see things as pointers to a wider horizon.

A bumper sticker reads "Born to Shop." In a society inclined toward consumerism, the healing power of poverty is crucial. Without poverty of spirit, affluence may sever people from any connection to the Sacred. Once basic needs, as for food, clothing and shelter, are fulfilled, then what? Is our destiny only to become greedy consumers? Or are we called to rise beyond this preoccupation?

The pressure to consume whatever presents itself as attractive leads to forgetfulness of the beyond in the midst of everydayness. A mindless personality lives mainly for material satisfaction. Commitment is scattered by the passion for possession. It is lost in concern for commodities.

Poverty of spirit is an invitation to rise above possessiveness. It enables us to become committed Christians. As such we can live in an affluent or indigent society with equal charity, peace and joy.

The challenge is to resist commercial pressure while still being involved in the world. The solution is to distance ourselves sufficiently from commercialism so that we can select more freely what fosters our unique call and commitment.

The mass media tempt people continually to become indiscriminate consumers. Production does not take into account spiritual needs, only growth of the economy. Irresponsible consumption may only produce a society of frustrated people who, without saying so, sense that their longing for the Sacred is neglected.

Perhaps never before in history has the spirit of poverty been so clearly a condition for the survival of a distinctively human culture, for at no other time were so many goods available and so many needs created by commercials in the media. This spirit enables us to transcend material goods as ultimate. It transforms matter by bringing out its spiritual meaning. It points to values hidden at its heart.

True artists go beyond the immediate appearance of matter and unveil its mystery. The seventeenth century Dutch painter, Nicholas Maes, and the twentieth century American, Andrew Wyeth, paint simple objects that are a part of our daily lives—a table setting, a fourposter bed, a basket of clothing—and faces we often see—laborers, fishermen, sailors. We have used these things and seen these people many times, yet, until we see them as the artist does, we may never suspect their mystery, never experience the silent meaning they evoke nor be able to share in the poverty of spirit which is the painter's.

Aesthetic vision expands in poverty. During the flowering of monastic life, a sense of beauty and graciousness prevailed. Medieval monasteries are still seen as places of aesthetic beauty. Visitors are awed by the architecture of the buildings, the sober way in which the monks planned their cells and corridors to maintain peace and solitude. Their handwritten and illustrated books prove that beauty and graciousness triumph over mere usefulness.

While living in the world as laity, we too must be able to transcend the tyranny of useful time, our addiction to production and indiscriminate consumption. Poverty of spirit encourages contemplation, prayer and recollection. To be poor in spirit is to live in readiness for the kind of detachment that enables our transcendent sensitivity to soar. Detached yet committed presence to God enables us to surpass what is merely pragmatic. Aesthetic experience, conditioned by poverty of spirit, creates a favorable atmosphere for seeing things in harmony with the deeper ground from which they emerge. This epiphanic sense of a higher consonance redeems things in our environment from isolation. They appear in a new light against the horizon of the Mystery which enfolds them. They speak to us in a new way, pointing to the greater whole in which we and they participate.

In a spirit of poverty, it becomes more possible for us to be aware of things as pointers to the Mystery, not merely products of mastery. This presence sustains both prayerful openness and a participative life of service. Worship and work cohere. We become an inspiration to others to seek God's face in the persons, events and things that make up their world.

### The Healing Power of Love

A third attitude of healing, sorely needed in today's world, is that of chaste or committed love. Chaste love of self and others is a love purified of egocentric impulses. Such threatening impulses tend to use self-love or love of others as a means of violating human dignity spiritually, psychologically or physically. While obedience tends to restore us to unity with unfolding reality, committed love tends to heal the break between individuals, cultures, races, creeds and religions.

Chaste love, committed and mature, enables us to affirm ourselves as God's creation. Paradoxically, the height of loving self-respect and commitment implies the depth of humility. The most profound act of humility implies full affirmation of the limited gifts of God that we are as well as commitment to the always limited life situations allotted to us.

The humility of respect for our unique limitations guards us from envying the unique calling of others. We do not strive in immature ways to keep up appearances that are alien to what we are. Neither do we force ourselves to accept a style of thought or feeling at odds with our calling. Unchaste self-rejection fragments us. It introduces standards, styles and ideals into our lives that are incompatible with who we are called to be. Unfortunately, many have not matured in the art of respectful listening to themselves and others. Children growing up in an overly organized society are especially in danger of forgetting who they are. They may adapt readily to streamlined customs, institutions and messages of the media they have not assimilated in their own way. It is almost impossible under these circumstances not to experience the dividing forces of disrespect and self-alienation. Therefore, we believe as Christians that only a deep and abiding self-appreciation, complemented by commitment, can heal these alienating forces in contemporary life.

Chaste, committed love fosters the other as other. It respects everyone's uniqueness and privacy. It promotes in humanity the best conditions for each person's harmonious unfolding. It strives to heal not only individual persons but also humanity as a whole.

Lacking such commitment, we may be tempted to level our relationships to stereotyped manifestations of superficial sympathy so typical of dehumanized crowds or collectivities. To escape the burden of responsibility mandated by mature love, we may resort to deceitful displays of pretended affection. We fear the solitude that is inseparable from the dignity of being a singular individual before God. We would rather hide in crowds that thrive on excited slogans.

Impersonal togetherness is a disintegrative force. It hampers our rise above crowd and collectivity to true community. Deep down we all desire that others will allow us to be who we are, that they will not overpower us with seductive opinions, exalted ideals and flaccid enthusiasms. In the core of our being we feel leery of clever and charming manipulators. We are wary of the power-strivings of disrespectful opinion makers and profane enthusiasts for so-called holy causes. We sense that their pious adherents would rob us of our personal inspiration. They threaten to dismiss us from their company if we do not flow blindly with their personal excitements.

As committed Christians, we must rise above the remnants of tribal collectivity. To stand free of the whims of the crowd, to stand forth as unique Christians, we must accept personal responsibility. Persons who respect one another will not easily be tricked into conformity by holding out the promise of in-group prestige and popularity.

A collectivity may disguise itself as a "community." What gives its true nature away is that respect for the dignity of persons in Christ is replaced by a glorification of the in-group as such. Respectful love resists the impulse to merge with an exclusive in-group. It feels repelled by the conformity and divisiveness it generates.

We can be faithful to the healing power of respectful love only if we recognize both the crowd and collectivity compulsion in ourselves. The tendency to hide in a crowd, clique or collectivity and to call it community is common in our society. Hence we are vulnerable. At every moment we can succumb to this pulsation. When we are least aware of it, we may fall back on the less than human level of submerging our individuality in the will of a make-believe community. Hence we must strive as committed Christians never to stay on the level of prepersonal togetherness.

All healing respect is rooted in growing awareness of the sacred ground from whence we emerge. Loving esteem for one another can heal the disfiguration that takes place in crowds, collectivities, cliques and make-believe communities. We must mature beyond this level of depersonalization. Discover your human dignity and experience anew conversion of heart and commitment to Christ, who calls you uniquely. Discover the same treasure in others. Respect the other as other in his or her particular commitments. This will create an atmosphere in which both of us can feel relaxed and unthreatened, confirmed and esteemed. This healing power may radiate outward to humanity at large. It may permeate society, increasing the moments in history in which personal love and true community will be valued and lived by increasing numbers of people for longer periods of time.

*Part Three*

*Love and Commitment*

## Chapter VIII

## Marital Love

Christian marriage represents the primary calling and course by which most Christians respond to God's inspiration. This sacrament is a striking confirmation of the spiritual capacity of two people, once strangers to each other, to commit themselves to an intimate and lasting togetherness out of which a family emerges. In the ritual that binds them "for better or worse," they vow to share their whole life with one another and with the children God may entrust to their care.

Marital intimacy overcomes egoism and gives new life to a couple. It represents the height of human encounter as it has evolved over the millennia in various cultures. Initially people were compelled to forge bonds of togetherness and build family compounds to survive in hostile surroundings. Genital relationships were of necessity motivated by the need for continuity of the clan or tribe. In many cultures marriages were pre-arranged to maintain the power and prestige of family groupings.

As conditions improved in societies, standards of living rose, spiritual ideals developed. An enlightened few were able to elevate marriage to a more exclusive and loving relationship. Gradually sexual needs were integrated into desires for loving togetherness, for home life and committed family ties. Marriage was no longer sought mainly as a means to promote projects like gathering food effectively, hunting or cultivating the land. It also became a way to show respect for each other's dignity and to facilitate growth for husband, wife and children.

In this context, Christian marriage can be seen as a symbol of the goodness and generativity each man and woman can bring to society, provided they are true to their vocation to love and respect one another and their children. However advanced their efforts are, they remain insufficient unless a couple's life together is illumined by the presence of Christ in humanity.

With the coming of Christ, the Holy Light entered into our world of flesh and made possible the divinization of humanity. Living as he did within his own immediate and extended family for the main part of his life, Jesus gave witness daily to the power of committed marital and familial love.

The presence of Christ in and with marriage partners grants to their relationship a depth and beauty undreamt of in the era of pre-Christian marriages. The sheer miracle that the Word was made flesh and dwells among us gives a new divine dimension to this most basic of bonds.

Growth in marital union and communion implies a twofold development of intimacy: love for oneself and devotion to one's spouse and children. Jesus taught that this love ought to guide people's relationships in general and marriage in particular. Christian marriage is the most intimate expression of the interwovenness of these two dimensions of love.

Christ makes both husband and wife aware of the worst and the best they can be for themselves and their families. This humble awareness of their limits must be complemented by a celebration of each other's gifts. Deepened togetherness contributes to a couple's daily sanctification. Each new situation they face, however challenging to their love and fidelity, lights up another facet of the diamond of their consecration. In communion with Christ, they learn from experience how his word can become flesh in their daily marital celebration.

## Living Commitment as Married Couples

The daily situations of work and play, laughter and tears, joy and pain, in which married people find themselves can disclose many hitherto unseen directives. The whispers of the Spirit are not only heard in holy places; they address obedient people in bedrooms, kitchens, dens, backyards and basements, provided they have ears to hear, eyes to see, and religious imaginations to interpret what is going on. Over the years, if a marriage is also a meeting place with God, spouses refine their radar, as it were, for what the Spirit may communicate through moments as common as tucking a child in bed or as rare as buying a new car or winning the lottery. The Holy Spirit, whose grace is everywhere, can use any and all events as channels of love in one's heart, of light to one's mind.

Parents and children cannot find their unique destiny by focusing on themselves in isolation from the larger community in which they live. Town, neighborhood, parish, workplace—all play a role in our growth. We must listen to what transpires in our own hearts, but this listening must be done in interaction with what is occurring around us. To hear the message of the beyond in the midst of everydayness, we must be willing in concrete ways to be our brothers' and sisters' keepers. To become involved as dedicated, caring persons, we must be detached from one-sided opinions and blind prejudices. This detachment disentangles us from duplicity. It corrects envious interpretations that obscure the light of the Spirit. Detachment tempers the tendency to impose our will on the feelings and aspirations of other family members, neighbors and friends. It allows us to hear the voice of the Spirit speaking in every child, youth and adult we encounter.

Allowing the inspirations of the Spirit to become a guiding force in family life calls for stillness inwardly and simplicity outwardly. We do not need complex nets to capture divine inspirations. They are free for the taking. Stillness and simplicity counteract anxious self-scrutiny. Such self-examination, and the image of an avenging God it generates, obscures the path an Eternal Love beckons us to tread lightly.

To become a family that sets its members free to find their own spiritual path, we must be willing to transcend harsh, demanding styles of relating and develop instead a firm and gentle approach. Gentleness generates an atmosphere in which family members create space for one another to mature. Together they become sensitive to the Divine Source in which all are rooted as a family. When we pray, we ask for the grace to see each moment of marital and family life as an epiphany or appearance of Divine Love.

Creative fidelity to the marriage vow also implies firmness. Couples must try to be honestly present to the thoughts, feelings and concerns they have to face together. Are their inner reactions true to the meaning of what happens here and now or are they a repetition of expectations held before marriage? Ingrained prejudices of the past may set the standards by which one judges a current situation. These expectations may reinforce defenses and distance spouses from one another.

Faithfulness to their commitments as married persons means that spouses vow to listen to what is going on in their daily life together and to let that input become the basis of honest dialogue. They must not allow fear of what may be said about past deformations, present problems or future dreams to mar the open communication that must characterize a Christian marriage.

Such inner fidelity is not easy to obtain. Perception, even of the beloved, is colored by impulses, ambitions and ideals one may have seen acted out or discussed in childhood, in families, in circles of colleagues or friends. It is difficult enough to listen to one another when all is going well; it is doubly difficult to do so when painful disclosures have to be made, crises faced, arguments settled, differences of opinion resolved. But such is the "stuff" of which marriage and family life is made. Through it all, one discerns the call of Christ to work for the glory of God and the good of each family member.

## *In Praise of Everydayness and Intimacy in Marriage*

No marriage is perfect. Each has its limitations. It is as wrong to idealize marriage as to underestimate its possibilities. Couples should be convinced that their marriage, with its particular difficulties, is also a field in which lies buried the pearl of maturation in holiness.

Absorption in "what could have been" makes it more difficult for couples to be present appreciatively to the pedestrian details of the here and now. Yet the actual situation is the fertile field where a marriage commitment has to mature or face stagnation.

Christian marriage cannot exist outside of the humdrum of everyday life—the hidden life of Nazareth. It is this reality that makes the family in truth a domestic church. The spirituality of marriage means facing the dreariness of everydayness in the light of the Formation Mystery. By meeting everyday demands with joy and courage, spouses are less in danger of becoming captives of the romantic dreams of marriage and family life portrayed by some writers or film makers. Could we get behind the scenes, we would soon stumble over the same problems and difficulties. These may be glossed over in print or media productions, but they are still there.

To be committed to the reality of marriage in and with Christ raises significantly one's chances of finding and growing in a mature love. Each of us is called in faith to open ourselves to the divine energies that fill the universe as well as our small niche in history. Openness on the plane of faith means that we are not trapped in desires to push beyond the pace of grace as given in a particular marriage. By the same token, openness empowers each spouse and child to develop their potentials without abuse, injury or undue violation of other family members.

True spirituality in marriage means that partners are no longer victims of fads and choices out of tune with their commitments. Remaining true to the simple joys of everydayness relieves couples from the need to recharge exalted feelings at the expense of failing to fulfill the promises and responsibilities that mutual care demands.

Lived in a wholly committed manner, marital love means that no affection for another human being can become more compelling than the love for one's marriage partner. The pledge of marital love always obliges spouses to limit their involvement with others if this would be detrimental to the priority of their love for spouse and family. It is to them that the married Christian is primarily committed.

The mere fact of physical presence together is not enough to keep a marriage alive. A married couple must foster relaxed, warm and loving concern for one another.

Modern society, with its highly competitive and rationalized procedures of labor and leisure, offers few sanctuaries for them to retire quietly as a couple or even alone. They must usually be content with evening hours or weekends. If they fill even these times exclusively with other interests, their loving commitment to one another and by extension to their children may be in danger of erosion.

Family life is fraught with disappointments. Limits, losses and failures can block intimacy or benefit maturation. Responding to limits in faith and love protects couples from living in illusion. The actual value of their marital consecration depends on what they are willing to give to one another in the present moment, not yesterday, not tomorrow, but today. Not to participate with care and courage in the day-to-day unfolding of married life is to miss the formative meaning manifested in the "sacrament of everydayness."

Tender gestures, loving words, patient evaluations of a problem, dealing with death and disease—all such acts and experiences are rich with affections, memories and decisions, with the weight of failure or the uplift of effectiveness. Marriage is a tapestry of such diverse decisions, experiences, insights and directives.

A couple's initial *yes* to this lasting life form is steadily renewed when they confront changing situations with courage. Each new *yes* is more and more ladened with wisdom and clarity. Each *yes* confirms and renews initial commitment. Fresh motivations—elevated by grace—empower married people to discover new directives in tune with their current situation and eternal calling.

To be faithful to their commitment, a couple must not fixate on what worked in the past. They must keep rejuvenating their consecration in the present. A marriage lived routinely could strangle love. It needs the repeated revival of the lovers' pledge of fidelity.

Fidelity in family life means using each limit as an opportunity to renew one's initial *yes*. It means generating energy each day through mutual responsiveness to directives springing from the here and now situation. The joy of commitment, characteristic of the first moment of choice, must increase, not cease, in the ups and downs of family life.

In and through creative fidelity, a marital consecration gains in strength and flexibility. It can bend with the winds of change without breaking. What supports such fidelity is the growing conviction that it is precisely within the marital life form that the partners shall find their unique direction, their true selves hidden in God. In this way, they learn to live with limits as signs of grace, as potential avenues to sanctification. A sense of duty, of mere obligation, is not enough to keep a marriage alive. It may give rise to an austere perseverance, stale and tedious. Such a relationship cannot be a joyful inspiration for the Christian community. To become chained to the marital life form, imprisoned by it like felons "doing time," is far from a Christian ideal. Couples living this treadmill of marriage may need spiritual guidance or counseling to be liberated and introduced anew to a loving and lively dialogue with daily situations as sources of new directives.

Being faithful does not mean being encapsulated in the past; it always implies an openness to the surprises of life today. They may appear less romantic and idealistic than one expected on the altar. They may seem to be pedestrian and earthly, but what else besides the everyday can nourish fidelity? Most commitments are lost or broken because one or the other partner fails to reap the fruits of dialogue with the daily situation. After a long period of neglect, people are no longer able to harmonize the demands of married life with ever new directives, limits and challenges emerging from successive life situations. They lose the facility for discovering new motives to keep their marriage alive.

*Today* is what counts in marriage and family life. Therefore, let us conclude this chapter with a hymn to everydayness written by Jerome Le Doux entitled "Today Is Everything."

> Every day is a new season all its own, for it transcends the sameness as well as the changes of spring, summer, fall and winter.
> Each day is a new reason. No matter what foreboding, negative or tragic things have happened on any preceding day, this day has its own raison d'être, goals and means.
> Every day is a fresh start. It is not only the beginning

of the rest of our life, but may very well be the only day which remains to us of our brief sojourn on earth.

Because we are so limited in mind and body, each day is all and more than we can handle, absorb, understand and appreciate.

Every day is a mouthful and often more than we can swallow, for "sufficient for the day is the evil thereof" (Mt. 6:34).

Each day is all that we can possess, as tomorrow rapidly becomes today and before today fades into yesterday.

Every day is a new faith in the meaning of life, and a new hope that we shall find, retain and be nourished by that meaning.

For better or for worse, each day is a new leaf in the book of life, and sometimes it is a whole new chapter.

Every day is a new treasure, perhaps not in gold or property, but surely in the riches of the heart, mind and emotions.

Each day is a new pleasure. Even where there is pain and sickness, we can live immersed in peace of mind and soul.

Each day is a distinct blessing from on high, a precious gift bursting forth from the immense love of God.

Each day is a new light, affording sharper and different views of ourself, our neighbor and of life itself.

Every day is a new excitement, as all nature works anew within us and around us the amazingly ordinary wonders of life.

Each day is a new growth, an expansion of the whole material universe outside of us and of our own microcosm inside of us.

Every day is an improvement, a becoming, for though we are not yet what we ought to be, we are far better than we used to be.

Each day is a new love, not lessening or destroying the old love of yesterday but increasing and deepening it.

Every day is a new path on which to strike out, a new vehicle by which to travel, a new source of energy for us to operate.

Each day is a new opportunity to correct the mistakes of yesterday and to deal with the challenges that face us now.

Each day is a new balance which enables us to dovetail the past with the present and to put everything into focus.

Each day is Christmas, since we have been joined by a Soul Brother who brought us the privilege of transcendent life.

Every day is New Year's Day, for it is today that we begin an entirely new life cycle in body, mind and soul.

There are no yesterdays except in history. There are no tomorrows except in hope. We can't afford to sit on our laurels of yesterday or foolishly bury ourselves in resentment over its bitterness. Neither can we afford to anticipate our successes of tomorrow, for tomorrow is not ours to count.

Each day is really all there is, though that is not an excuse simply to eat, drink and make merry. Yesterday is a cancelled check. Tomorrow is a promissory note. But today is cash.

# Chapter IX

# Romantic Love—
# Prelude to Committed Love

Some of us may experience at certain moments the heady experience of romantic love. However animating this may be, we realize sooner or later that it is bound to end. Still this experience is stirring, even overwhelming, for many.

Each of us wants to escape loneliness and isolation, the fear of being unlovable. Eternal Love has instilled in us a longing to go beyond ourselves, to participate in the mystery of intimacy. When we feel thrown back on ourselves, out of touch with others, we suffer anxiety and depression. Our whole life is a yearning for participation in that which is "more than" we are. Such is the distinctive mark of human transcendence. We are in some way always "more than" we seem. This longing impels us to find intimacy with a beloved, who represents the "more than" for us in some way.

To live a spiritual life is to surpass continually what we are by sharing in the countless epiphanies of God's love that shine forth in the everyday world. Any personal encounter is a meeting with that special epiphany of God manifested on earth—the human person. God comes nearer to us in and through human encounters in depth. As a contemporary song says, "To love another person is to see the face of God." Such a meeting personalizes for us our aspiration for participation in an all-perfect, infinitely tender Holy Other. The loving mystery discloses itself in a multiplicity of manifestations—most effectively in a friend, a sweetheart, a husband, wife or child, a mother, father or grandparent.

## *Falling in Love*

When we fall in love with someone, we may experience the temporary ecstasy of romantic affection. This gifted moment may remind us of the attraction of love divine. So fascinated are we that we may be blinded at that moment to each other's imperfections, forgetting that the woman or man we encounter in young, excited love is but a limited and imperfect epiphany of the divine mystery.

The person who evokes this unique experience may appear to us as the ideal image of Woman or Man. She or he may even mirror for us the eternal idea of womanhood or manhood held in the mind of God. The Beatrice of Dante or the Prince in the fairy tale of Cinderella may be popular pointers to that idealized image in our imagination of the perfect feminine or masculine. The other no longer seems only a particular individual with limits and strengths; the other becomes the personification of this eternal image as it lives in our fantasy.

How can the romantic experience serve the unfolding of a Christian's spiritual life? Romantic love is not permanent. It can be beautiful, but it is also of brief duration. Its fleeting intensity in and by itself cannot promise lasting fulfillment. Still the rapture that may stir the heart and soul of many people has inspired song and celebration in every century and in all cultures. Romantic love should point to a more profound possibility for those aroused by its sweet melody. It must receive its ultimate sense not from itself but from a higher form of love.

## Gift of Romantic Love

First of all, romantic love may awaken a person to a crucial awareness. Lifelong dedication to a beloved spouse and family of one's own does provide a way to share in God's own love for those to whom one is committed. Romantic experience—and the discovery involved in it—may suddenly lift a person out of isolation. The experience of falling in love may even be for some the first avenue of escape from sheer loneliness.

Romantic experience can evoke the silent or spoken sense that the beloved is also a pointer to a divine mystery. Every attraction, exalted charm and beauty beheld in the beloved can reflect God's idea of the ideal form or essence of manhood or womanhood. Delight and wonder in reference to the goodness of the beloved are felt time and again. This special feeling may linger on even when the glow of romantic rapture dims. It dims when the limitations of mere humanness combine with the sobriety of mundane existence.

The lover may experience the beloved as called by the Spirit to approximate the image of womanhood or manhood God has in mind from all eternity. This insight should remain after the message of romantic love passes away. It becomes an appeal to realize ever anew the unique selves we are before God, in other words, to reflect God's loving idea of who and what one is. Hence the best remnant of romantic love is the readiness to grow to love the other in a lifelong commitment.

Anne Morrow Lindbergh writes in her meditative book, *Gift from the Sea:*

> For the first part of every relationship is pure, whether it be with friend or lover, husband or child. It is pure, simple and unencumbered. It is like the artist's vision before he has to discipline it into form, or like the flower of love before it has ripened to the firm but heavy fruit of

responsibility. Every relationship seems simple at its start. The simplicity of first love, or friendliness, the mutuality of first sympathy seems, at its initial appearance—even if merely in exciting conversation across a dinner table—to be a self-enclosed world.

. . . And then how swiftly, how inevitably the perfect unity is invaded; the relationship changes; it becomes complicated, encumbered by its contact with the world. I believe this is true in most relationships, with friends, with husband or wife, and with one's children. But it is the marriage relationship in which the changing pattern is shown up most clearly because it is the deepest one and the most arduous to maintain; and because, somehow, we mistakenly feel that failure to maintain its exact original pattern is tragedy (Pantheon Edition, 1955, pp. 64–66).

## Conditions for Committed Love

Romantic love as such does not imply a lasting commitment. Moreover, many married people enjoy a lifelong and loving, mutual commitment without the prelude of romantic fascination. As the initial enchantment comes to an end, it may point beyond itself to a deeper calling. It may serve as an overture to share one's life lastingly with that of the beloved. Once the prelude of romantic love has illuminated a relationship and redeemed one from loneliness, the stage may be set for the commitment of marital love. The early stages of the transition may prove to be somewhat melancholic. Romance may fade already before the fullness of marital love is experienced. According to Lindbergh:

> It is true, of course, the original relationship is very beautiful. Its self-enclosed perfection wears the freshness of a spring morning. Forgetting about the summer to come, one often feels one would like to prolong the spring of

early love, when two people stand as individuals, without past or future, facing each other. One resents any change, even though one knows that transformation is natural and part of the process of life and its evolution. Like its parallel in physical passion, the early ecstatic stage of a relationship cannot continue always at the same pitch of intensity. It moves to another phase of growth which one should not dread, but welcome as one welcomes summer after spring (*ibid.*, p. 66).

If there is an unrealistic aspect of romantic love, it pertains to a kind of blindness to the limitations of the beloved. This results from a tendency to identify the imperfect epiphany of the Mystery, which our beloved is, with his or her ideal form in God. We can idolize the beloved without realizing that this person, however special, is only a blemished image of God's eternal idea of his or her uniqueness. The everyday unfolding of committed marital love reveals only too clearly that the other is only a vulnerable human person.

Growth in marital love entails a transformation of romantic love, enabling us to go beyond our absorption in one another. In the words of Antoine Saint-Exupery: "Love does not consist in gazing at each other but in looking outward together in the same direction."

Romantic love comes to those temperamentally disposed to receive it as a gift, an unexpected surprise. In itself it does not oblige one to make a permanent commitment; it only points the way. In the romantic phase of love, exalted expectations are not yet disappointed. But without suffering or sacrifice, our inner resources are not easily mobilized. For this reason sheer romance does not transform our life in depth.

Romantic love manifests itself mainly in the emotional and aesthetic spheres of our personality. It can be an appeal to the best in us, yet it remains open to something more. It does not necessarily penetrate the deeper regions of the heart where true commitments are born and grow.

If we persist in the quest for romantic love alone, we may delay our chances for maturation. Maturation implies a call to commitment, arising from the depths of our heart. In the mysterious center of our life, the Spirit draws us to decide whether or not to establish a family of our own with this unique person. Romantic love is thus a question rather than an answer, a mutual idealization rather than a promise of permanent care. Committed marital love is a vow to serve lastingly each other's unique unfolding within the realistic boundaries of family and society.

Committed marital love is for most, if not all, the way to fulfill the highest aspirations of human life: to receive and give form to Divine Love, consonantly and sacrificially, within the intimacy and social outreach of one's own family. Marital love represents commitment *par excellence* because it directs us to forego whatever is incompatible with caring for a family of our own. Inwardly, this commitment sparks in us a readiness to submit our actions, thoughts and feelings to the primary responsibility for family care. Outwardly, life begins to revolve around this commitment so that we take it into account whatever we do.

Love lived in commitment to marriage and family life is vastly different from the feelings of vital affection that romantic love may engender. Committed marital love is a way of life for the couple concerned; it is the basis of their family-centered spirituality. Abandoning their autonomous existence, two become as one and share fully in the manifold joys and sorrows that life together brings to them.

This surrender, inspired by the Spirit, does not mean loss of one's uniqueness, personal judgment, or acceptance of responsibility. At times lively disagreement may be as common as lively agreement. The thoughts, decisions and plans that direct one's actions are no longer developed solely in the light of "What is good, useful, or interesting for me?" but "What is good, useful, or interesting for us?" or "What benefits the family for which we together are responsible?"

This commitment of our whole being is never finished or perfect. It is frequently discontinued and at times threatened. Divorce and the plight of infidelity are obvious examples of what can happen without the cultivation of commitment. Feelings, thoughts, fantasies, urges and desires emerge suddenly to challenge our integrity. We cannot force them to conform indiscriminately to our good intentions. Therefore, our option "to be for the other," though pledged once and for all in the core of our being, can only gradually expand its influence to the peripheral regions of emotions, expectations and actions.

The commitment of marital love does not mean that we shall always maintain a fever pitch of attraction for the other or that we will always "feel" our love or not be tempted to betray it. There will be times when we feel angry, when we quarrel and fight, kiss and make up. Temptation, divisiveness, impatience and other sources of division may paralyze and even extinguish romantic love whereas these same setbacks can solidify the meaning of commitment. This is so because romantic love resides chiefly in the borderline regions of our personality, in the realm of vital passions and warm feelings. Yet the same emotional upsets will not directly destroy marital love, which maintains its integrity in the committed core of our personality.

The Holy Spirit grants to couples living a solid marital commitment the grace to transform these borderline regions of irritation and resistance. By means of the promises made to one another in the sacrament of matrimony, they draw upon original blessings. The grace of this sacrament implies the readiness to restore deep love whenever its expression is impaired or threatened by dissension and misunderstanding. It fosters also the willingness to overcome temptations to infidelity, doubt, seduction or manipulation of one's partner. Sacramental commitment becomes deeper and stronger every time we are called to reaffirm it in the face of dissonance. The same disagreements and disillusions that might destroy romantic love serve to strengthen committed love by fostering a renewed *yes* to one's marriage vows.

Marital love grows stronger in adverse situations, leading finally to that unshakable, solid quality of love that so often impresses us in aging people. They have matured in commitment over a lifetime of working through family tensions. Their love has been tested and proved a hundred times over. They know that setbacks are powerless to wreck the vows they made to one another. Cultural pulsations preach that broken promises are par for the course. Aging couples belie this conclusion. They witness to the serene conviction that disagreements and irritations cannot erode the rock of their commitment. The house of their marital love is not built on the quicksand of romantic feelings but on the solid ground of grace. They may at times quarrel or complain about each other. Yet they would prefer any irritability of their company to the betrayal of their love. Inspired by their commitment to one another before God, they are steadily disposed to bind up wounds and heal differences.

In his novel *The Idiot*, Fyodor Dostoyevsky describes the love between General Yepanchin and his wife as an example of the durability of committed love. Romance may be missing from this encounter but real and lasting love is surely there.

> Sometimes she [Mrs. Yepanchin] asked her husband about it [the foolishness of their youngest daughter, Aglya] and, as usual, waited hysterically and peremptorily for his answer. General Yepanchin hummed and hawed, knit his brow, shrugged his shoulders, and at least, spreading out

his hands in a perplexed gesture, gave his opinion: "She needs a husband!"

"Only God grant he's not like you, sir," Mrs. Yepanchin at last exploded like a bomb.

"Not like you, sir, in his opinions and judgments. Not a coarse fellow like you sir!" General Yepanchin promptly made his escape, and Mrs. Yepanchin calmed down after her "explosion." The same evening, needless to say, she infallibly became particularly attentive, gentle, affectionate, and respectful to her husband, her coarse fellow, her kind, dear and adored Ivan Fyodorovich, for she had been fond of him, and even in love with him all her life, which General Yepanchin knew very well himself and he respected her greatly for it (Penguin Books Edition, 1955, p. 365).

*Chapter X*

# Dispositions of Committed Marital Love

The stronger and deeper their sacramental commitment is, the more spouses can allow themselves to engage in creative dissent with one another. The more exclusively romantic their love is, as some pre-marital bondings show, the more disastrous any serious disagreement or critique will seem.

Marital love does not imply—as does romantic love—that one always consciously experiences how much in love one is. The feeling tone of love may be momentarily suspended, especially following a fight. In that case, one's sacramental commitment finds expression in the fact that both partners agree deep down to seek again the restoration of harmony between them and in their family. Some couples may even pledge not to go to bed unless peace between them is restored.

This fundamental readiness manifests itself in four basic dispositions: acceptance, surrender, fidelity and creative care.

The disposition of *acceptance* guarantees on the part of the couple a permanent readiness to take one another as they are. Not every personality trait can be known, no matter how lengthy the friendship or courtship may be. Lovers manage to surprise one another. The many sides of their personalities become known in the varied life situations they encounter together. Certain trying circumstances may draw out characteristics unsuspected by the partners. What we can hide in public life becomes obvious in private. We cannot conceal the nuances of our personality from the person with whom we live day after day, year after year. Here again the grace of sacramental commitment enables married people to accept each other. They give each other space and time to grow, even when they are taken aback by hitherto hidden facets of their personalities. Their commitment is fundamentally to the graced potential goodness of their partner, even when the storms of life cloud the best qualities they beheld or fancied at the beginning of their relationship.

The disposition of *surrender* suggests a willingness to grow in spiritual maturity so that the gift each person is may bloom before the face of the Most High. One can only surrender to another gifts acquired through cooperation with grace. To grow in self-understanding and subsequent self-formation together is not easy. Understanding and forming the whole persons we are is the task of a lifetime. The worthwhileness of mutual surrender depends on a willingness to engage in continual maturation. If one person stagnates, so may the other.

Self-surrender in this context means putting our best self at the disposal of the other. It would be disastrous if such surrender were to be misunderstood as an enslavement to arbitrary whims. This kind of game-playing can only harm a couple's capacity to realize God's project for their life. Readiness to investigate the source of every failure in self-surrender and maturity makes loving spouses more sensitive to their hidden defenses. They begin to detect their pre-focal anxieties, their stubborn withholding of themselves.

Lurking hostilities, distrust, bitterness and a host of human failings threaten the art of relating. Such weaknesses do not render impossible the love of sacramental commitment. Problems like these may only impair temporarily its flowering.

True marital love, as the expression goes, conquers all. It implies the readiness to alter gradually in oneself what may be an obstacle to mutual surrender. This readiness may not succeed in changing actions and attitudes. This does not mean that commitment has failed. Only when the willingness to improve is absent from a shaky relationship, the dynamism of love is bound to be impaired.

The disposition of *fidelity* belongs to the essence of committed love. Without loyalty, marital love becomes impossible. Whether in health or sickness, success or failure, excitement or dreariness, harmony or discord, an unyielding commitment to remain faithful to one's sacramental vows should prevail.

Fidelity in everyday life means that loving spouses will start to work without delay on their attitudes toward one another when their relationship is threatened. The minute they discover their love weakening for lack of communication, their mutual presence becoming stale, stilted or endangered by extra-marital temptations, they go to work.

At times fidelity may involve the willingness to seek psychotherapy, marriage counseling or spiritual direction. The same disposition creates a condition of vigilance against so much absorption in other interests—like careerism, social climbing, study, sports, hobbies, charitable enterprises and socializing—that a couple cannot preserve tender attention to their own needs and those of their children. No way of involvement may become so predominant that it interferes with primary care for one's family. Therefore, Christian husbands or wives remain wary of becoming so over-involved in relationships or activities outside their marriage that in effect they are committing a kind of adultery. Basically they are betraying the fidelity that has to flow from a sacramental commitment to the beloved as the first person of worth in one's life without neglecting the obligations of social outreach beyond one's family.

The disposition of *creative care* connotes a readiness to

foster the vital, functional and social conditions that will facilitate the unique growth of the other. Examples would be provisions for each other's health maintenance, recreational needs and social well-being. This kind of care is creative. Faith in the beloved's potential for good reveals itself also in gentle solicitation for the other's spiritual development too. In view of the nature of committed love, we can better appraise the place and limits of romantic love.

## The Limits of Romantic Love

When romantic love follows its proper course, there are only two possible answers to its invitation: to extend or not to extend it to a commitment for life. Either response may be right, depending on the situation. We may discover that the man or woman who attracted us romantically is not the person we are called to commit our life to unconditionally and forever. We may realize, on the contrary, that he or she is that one person meant for us. Then we may decide to bind our lives in lasting, marital commitment. In that case romantic love would have fulfilled its purpose in a man or woman's formation journey. As romantic, the love becomes less central. It will be gradually embedded in and transformed by mature marital love, in short, by commitment.

Romantic love, despite its promise, can become inauthentic when its relative diminishment meets with too much resistance on the part of a couple. When the role of romantic love as partial and temporary is not accepted, it can become a hindrance instead of a help. This delightful fascination, if aimed exclusively at itself, at romance for romance's sake, will deteriorate. In some instances life may be reduced to a cultivation of romantic mood swings with no basis in reality and no complement in commitment.

This degenerated form of romantic love does not lift us

beyond ourselves. It does not widen and deepen our lives. We become entrapped in a self-centered universe of feelings and affections. We do not find lasting communion with God through commitment to the beloved. Rather we find only our own unhappy self, starved for realistic communion in depth. This is the goal that persistently eludes us as we chase an impossible dream. Having lost its meaning in the realm of appeal, romantic love becomes a fantasy, an illusion.

The desperate search for a lasting, exclusively romantic love can take many forms. It is an increasingly common deviation in western culture. Its frequency may be due to a general immaturity, to the exaltation of romanticism in movies, novels, commercials, and to a penchant for postponing adulthood by delaying adolescence. Many unhealthy elements in our society may inhibit maturation in human love, the most obvious being an inability to make a permanent commitment.

In later chapters we shall analyze further deformative elements in our society. We can only point out here that one of the main characteristics of western deformation is scientism. This *ism*, not science as such, overemphasizes the functional skills and cognitions enabling us to conquer, control and organize the world around us, but often at the cost of keeping us infantile in regard to inner maturation in love and commitment.

Many persons raised in the west are not ready for the committed love of marriage and friendship. Their one-sided development has left them crippled in the area of commitment. Unprepared for committed love, yet starving for human communion, they fall back on the fascinating and endless cycle of the "seduce and conquer" mentality typical of the idealization of romantic love affairs. When romantic love degenerates in this way, it loses its inner orientation toward God and the other. One forgets that God's implicit self-disclosure in the epiphany of the other is the hidden source of the sublimity of romantic love and its preparation for commitment.

Romantic love, if not complemented in time by some form of committed love, cannot last. As a result a substitute pseudo-love takes over. The sensual part of the romantic experience then becomes its exclusive content. The compulsive striving of some sensitive lonely persons for romantic love may decay into a kind of addiction to sentimentality, instant intimacy and periodic thrills. This compulsion may be kept burning by uncommitted sex and various forms of promiscuous behavior that in the end leave a person terribly empty, more alone and unloved than ever.

The sick tendencies of a culture, as well as its healthy leanings, are embedded in popular myths. These shape the pre-focal ideals of sizable groups of the population, young, middle-aged and old. Cultural myths promoting exclusive sensuality cut off from commitment are kept alive by the media, including magazines, novels, musical lyrics, theater dramas and a never ending stream of fads and fashions.

## *Fallacies of Romantic Love*

One prevalent cultural myth is that of the exclusive importance of romantic love. A host of fallacies make up this myth. We shall identify four of them here.

A first fallacy of the myth of romantic love is the suggestion that romantic pleasure represents the highest possible fulfillment of human life. The consequences of buying into this fallacy can be disastrous. The implicit suggestion that the very possibility of love is gone when romantic rapture wears off may lead to a feverish search to feel the former ecstasy with a new person every time. Every new relationship may for a while enable the lover to identify the beloved with an idealized image of perfect womanhood or manhood. But one discovers sooner or later that the new lover, too, is only a limited manifestation of the mystery of the "More Than." The myth of romantic love again drives one headlong into another temporary relationship where the same sad story repeats itself.

Another fallacy engendered by this myth is that marital love would ideally be the continuation of only the romantic aspect of human love. This attitude may lead to a stubborn determination to identify one's spouse with the idealized image of what the perfect mate would be like. The myth in this form breaks the cardinal rule that love means affirming each other as imperfect points of departure toward what we are called to become, according to our eternal form in the Divinity. This love implies a sharing in responsibility for the other's becoming what he or she is uniquely called to be. Fixation on only the romantic aspect of love within marriage fosters unrealistic expectations. A couple soon becomes self-centered instead of partner-centered. Such narcissism leads inevitably to disillusionment, to feeling cheated, resisted, resentful and hostile.

A third fallacy evoked by the myth is that of the mysterious "only possible one" with whom alone we could establish a marital commitment. Even when people have been married for many years, the dream of the "only possible one" may suddenly begin to haunt their memory and imagination, tempting them away from their marriage commitment. In the process, the spouses or even couples who are dating may overlook the treasure they really have. True marital love must grow on the basis of stable bonding, not on romantic fascination alone. There are many persons to whom one could commit oneself. An actual marital commitment means that one vows to stay faithful to one person, no matter how many others may seem romantically attractive. Every other attitude but that of mature fidelity would be a contradiction to the essence of sacramental commitment. It would interfere with one's spiritual growth in and through marriage by repeated affirmation of one's original *yes* in times of doubt and temptation. Clearly such a stance is counter-cultural, but it alone protects one from becoming the victim of this or any other fallacy of romantic love.

To keep feeding the romantic fantasy of the mysterious "only possible one" may lead to serious difficulties. What if the victim of this myth meets a person who arouses his or her romantic sensitivity? If no romantic love was experienced in or before one's own marriage, and, still more seriously, if the cultivation of the love of commitment was neglected, the temptation may be overwhelming. Marriages may break apart on this basis alone.

A lasting fallacy of the myth of the exclusivity of romantic love is the false notion that a marriage cannot be happy unless it is initiated by high-pitched romantic fascination. The core of mature love is the total graced commitment that a couple makes to one another's spiritual formation. This commitment, illumined by grace, unites both partners unconditionally to one another. Then the love between them can grow strong and beautiful, even if they encountered each other originally on the basis of sincere motives other than those of romantic love.

Committed love is gift in its purest form, a gift readily given to those who are open with their whole being to its arrival. True love presupposes lasting openness to the manifold epiphanies of the divine mystery. The most evident epiphany may be for us that special person sent by God to share our journey in the spiritual and physical intimacy of a marital relationship.

## Integration of the Married Life

If marital love is true, it will deepen over the years, granting meaning and substance to all the things a husband and wife do together, from paying bills, washing dishes and changing diapers, to dining by candlelight, enjoying an evening at the theater and sharing prayer. Many husbands and wives find it difficult to maintain the transcendent aspect of their love and its joyous embodiment in everyday tasks and concerns. After a few years of marriage, their love may seem to fade, almost to disappear. The functions of daily life are no longer a delightful expression of their affection for each other and for their children. They have become a drudgery. Life grows empty and dreary. The beautiful inspiration of love no longer directs these little tasks, elevating them above the mundane level. The marital love that should integrate them seems to have burnt out in their tired hearts. At its worst, home becomes a dungeon to which they feel chained by marital and parental duties. They become prisoners of their own bitterness about the ideals that everyday life together has seemingly betrayed.

What is the meaning of this death of inspiration? Men and women caught in this dilemma are no longer able to be faithful to the rhythm of marital life—that of a recollected rekindling of love, celebrated before God, and spilling over in the formation of their daily physical, functional and spiritual lives. They may have become so preoccupied with necessary family, professional and social functions that they are unable to find special moments of recollection in which life and love come together again.

In moments of graced togetherness before the Eternal, their marital life may be seen anew in its sacramental light. The integrating ideals of a Christian marriage may once again shine through the drudgery of routine. Away from daily pressures, husband and wife may return to the joy of committed marital love. Space and time for integration restores togetherness and prevents marriage from becoming a collection of isolated duties without a unifying meaning. Recollection at the right moment enables couples to return to routine responsibilities radiant and renewed. Moments of marital everydayness can then be interwoven anew in the splendid mosaic of their sacramental commitment to one another and to their family.

## Chapter XI

# Marital Sexuality and Spirituality

Christian spouses cultivate an intimate relationship with God through intimacy with one another. Essential to marital maturity is sexual intimacy, responsible, generative, joyful. The more comfortable spouses are in their sexual encounters, the more they may develop a true marital spirituality. In union with God and with one another, they express through their bodies the love they feel in their hearts, a love graced by God's own eternal affection for them.

Despite this ideal, it seems as if a high number of married Christians do not experience their sexual life together as an avenue to spiritual deepening. They seem unable to integrate sexuality and spirituality. This is a major problem in adult Christian formation. To understand the disintegration that occurs, we must reflect on our bodily-sexual existence. It is only possible to get to the root of this problem if we consider the way in which our culture understands sexuality. What the media convey about sex, of course, affects Christians who live in this society.

From all sides, it is clear that sexuality has become a source of dissonance and disruption, not a wellspring of consonance and unity. Women are harassed, children are sold into pornography, so-called "open marriages" mock fidelity. This gift of God, to be lived fully in marital commitment, has been reduced to an isolated genital act referred to in common parlance as "it" (doing *it*, not doing *it*, doing *it* in the right or wrong way, doing *it* with whomever we can and whenever *it* is available). Rather than stressing the beautiful consonance of sexuality and spirituality, we have relegated these dimensions of life to separate compartments, reducing one to genitality and the other to a vague pietism with no connection to vital needs and potentials.

## *Sexuality as Dissonant*

Preoccupation with sexuality as mere genital performance often outweighs concern for other aspects of life. A one-sided fixation on "it" indicates that this facet of character formation is not as consonant with our whole personality as it ought to be. Therefore, we write and talk so much about "it." Similarly, we do not pay much attention to the water we drink until the source of supply is polluted by oil and chemicals. Then it becomes a main topic of conversation.

In other words, when any aspect of everyday life is no longer integrated into the entire flow of human maturing, it may draw excessive attention to itself. The same applies to our sexual life. When we hear some of the advice dispensed from popular commentators concerning human sexuality, we are struck by an excessive stress on mere genitality and the thrill of "instant intimacy."

Preoccupation with sexuality can also appear in another form, this one resulting in an over-abundance of rules and regulations. For example, one generation may insist that regardless of the occasion, even in marriage, full exposure of the body is always a menace to the spiritual meaning of sexuality. Extremists in the generation following may claim the opposite, saying nudity is acceptable under any circumstances. Both immoderate directives tend to isolate sexuality as a vehicle of bodily pleasure from spirituality.

In yet another instance, married Christians may be inundated with excessive warnings about the dangers of sexuality. Long before being able to appraise these cautions in a relaxed and realistic fashion, they may either rebel against them or adhere too strictly to them. Both extremes prevent reasoned assessment of what may really be moving them as persons. Have they taken such warnings out of context and turned them into rigid rules? Do they understand the need for time-honored traditions in the history of sexual-spiritual formation? Have they adopted these cautions in an appropriate manner? Have reminders about the dangers of sexuality or desires for its pleasures become more important to them than the value of loving sexual encounter in marital intimacy?

False notions about the nature of sexuality belie the basic tenets of the Christian tradition. The result of this deformation is a confused attitude toward sexuality as isolated from a fully human spirituality.

Long before couples face the challenge of growing toward an integrated, joyful sexuality in marriage, they have to face another fact. They bring into their relationship certain ideas and feelings about sex. As an adolescent, a man may never have worked through fears and misgivings about the engulfing forces that females symbolize in his life. A woman may wonder if she is still attractive, if she can express her erotic urges, if she can love without shame. In adolescence young people begin to experience powerful sexual desires. They do not know how to connect the wild frenzy of sexual longing with the belief systems associated with living a spiritual life. It takes time to integrate physical needs and desires—understood as a preparation for marital intimacy—with one's yearning for God. The problem is that some people carry over into marriage adolescent guilts, fears and fantasies that have not been worked through. They experience more tension than integration between the sexual and spiritual realms of their being. The formation of our sexual life takes place from infancy onward in interaction with parents or guardians. They communicate to us in words, gestures and actions what people commonly believe to be sexually right or wrong, acceptable or unacceptable. Initial formation never occurs in isolation from the assumptions, prejudices, cautions and actions of the adult representatives of a formation tradition. These representatives have filtered the directives of their tradition through their particular personality with its own limits, confusions and prejudices. What we learn from them, good and bad, harmful and helpful, stays with us well into married life.

Little children are faced with their parents' decisions and actions in this regard. What parents say and do is affected in turn by the view of sexuality prevalent in the culture and influenced by the way in which they were treated or mistreated by their parents. Statistics prove that abused children tend to be abusive in turn to their offspring.

No person is an island in the swirling sea of formation, especially not in the affective realm of bodily-sexual development. The initial assimilation of hurts and healing encounters is the most powerful factor one brings to marital intimacy. Both spouses carry into the marriage the pattern of sexuality instilled in them by their own family relations and traditions. If one spouse's "knapsack" is full of problems, if their family backgrounds are significantly different, conflicts between them as marriage partners will pose a challenge to Christian maturity.

Early childhood impressions in an abusive home, for instance, will be vastly at variance with those one receives in a loving atmosphere. In many cases, initial formation does not include the conviction that sexuality and spirituality are meant to form a natural and essential partnership both in and outside of marriage.

Problems of disagreement and mutual misunderstanding can only be solved if spouses take time to talk in an honest way about their divergent family backgrounds and feelings about sexual intimacy. For instance, a wife may have grown up in a warm, loving family where she received frequent hugs, touches and kisses from her parents. Her husband's experience may be the opposite. He was raised with parents who seldom, if ever, touched their children, preferring verbal contact and shying away from physical expression. This couple will have to face up to these differences in childhood formation if their marital intimacy is to satisfy the wife and help to heal the husband of lingering feelings of coldness and an unlovable self-image.

The Christian tradition to which the couple is committed should facilitate critical and creative appraisal of the factors that have formed their thoughts and feelings toward sexuality. In the presence of Christ, a troubled couple may be able to understand better basic directives pertaining to sexuality and spirituality and the particular way in which these were communicated in their families. They may become aware that the general Christian commandment to love and be loved was lived out in an anxious or frigid way. Such fears may have led to loveless, withdrawn dispositions followed by erratic outbursts of lustful passion. The mistake is to identify unwholesome expressions of human sexuality with the foundational directives behind them.

Consider, for example, a pious Christian woman whose marriage is sexually defective and unfulfilling. Frigidity of mind and body interferes with her hidden hope for spontaneous sexual intimacy. She may engage in intercourse while feeling deep down that the sexual act itself is despicable. Her depreciative attitude may be rooted in a misinterpretation of the moral principles governing marriage as these were communicated in her family. Rules were imposed on her so arbitrarily that she concluded sexuality in itself must always be slightly mean and dirty, not really in accord with God's plan but at most a duty. If she risks deeper reflection with her husband or seeks marriage counseling, she may become aware that this conclusion is not justifiable, that it is not even in the Bible. She may see that other pious Christian women, raised in the same church as herself and subjected to the same directives communicated in a healthier way by their families, did not become frigid. Further reflection may bring her to the insight that there must be something wrong with the way in which she chose to live out the directives of her faith tradition in marriage.

## *Sexuality as Consonant*

Christian spouses are called to commit themselves to a life of unitive and procreative sexuality that remains in tune with their spirituality. Sexuality remains fully human when they commit themselves to its expression in a vibrant as well as a chaste and respectful way. The meaning of the word "chaste" in the context of marital sexuality is often misunderstood in a narrow manner. It actually means, from the verb "to chasten," "to refine" or "to purify." It follows that the chastening of love in marriage makes possible its sexual expression purified from the self-centered, immature impulses that would use sex as a means of mere self-indulgence or dominance without regard for the needs and desires of one's partner and the moral precepts of the church.

Chaste, respectful love helps married people as well as those who are single to lift sexuality as a whole, instead of mere genitality, into the realm of spirituality where it receives its most distinctive human expression. Lack of respect in sexual encounter becomes, by contrast, a main source of dissonance. It mars intimacy and alienates spouses from one another.

Lack of loving respect is a disintegrating force in sexual intimacy. By contrast, chaste love in marriage is a disposition enabling couples to restore the spiritual integrity of sexual encounter and of their marital relationship as a whole. Respect in sexual encounter will then radiate into all aspects of their marital relationship.

Chaste, committed love means that men and women wholeheartedly accept their sexuality as a precious gift of the Spirit, fostering the consonance of their life together. Committed love enhances marital consonance by celebrating the other as other, also sexually, in all of her or his uniqueness. This disposition listens especially to the other's sexual needs and tries to fulfill these freely and generously in keeping with the plan of God. Chaste loving creates the best conditions for the unfolding of each other's sexual life both procreatively and unitively. It guarantees the best climate for family upbringing as well.

Respectful encounters in sexual intimacy reveal spouses to one another not only in their sexual potency and attractiveness, but also as unique manifestations of God's love within and around them. Each aspect of their being, especially the sexual, leaves its own imprint on character formation. Each is worthy of divinely inspired respect. This imprint is a gift of God. That is why in and through their love for one another spouses enhance their personal relationship with God—and with God manifested precisely in and through the gifts they bring to their sexual encounter.

Absence of chaste respect for the other's uniqueness will always tend to reduce a marital love relationship to superficial manifestations of sentimental affection or functional effectiveness. This kind of encounter rarely grows to the rapture of sexual-spiritual moments of sublime consonance of body and soul in unity with one another and with the Divine Mystery pervading and elevating human love.

To escape the disappointment of failed sexuality, spouses may resort to deceitful displays of pretentious love, shallow imitations of the real thing. Such impersonal, self-destructive togetherness, no matter how pronounced its idealization, is a divisive, disintegrative force eroding marriage and damaging its mature formation. It hampers the call to consonance. This call begins to emerge at the moment husband and wife confirm each other's uniqueness in the commonality of the marriage commitment. They may then rise above the superficiality of isolated genitality and celebrate in loving encounter the fully spiritual-sexual persons they are called to be by the Forming Mystery.

## Chapter XII

## Maturing in Christian Love

Whatever our age, status or state of life may be, we are called to love God above all else and to love others and ourselves in him. The way in which we love, bodily and spiritually, depends on whether we are married or single, young or old, sick or well. This variety of expression is a mark of human love as human. For example, the way a father loves his son or daughter is different from the way he loves his wife, his best friend and his parents. All love must be expressed in a manner that makes it real and acceptable within the situation in which we find ourselves—that of nurse to patient, parent to child, boyfriend to girlfriend, priest or minister to a congregation, and so on.

A human love life does not happen automatically. It begins in early childhood. Infants cannot dialogue with parents about their needs. They only know how to cry, even scream, if, for example, their diaper is wet or soiled. Children have no way of distinguishing between their unique identity and their wet bottom. It is as if the entire world has become nasty and damp and the entire world demands to be dry.

The immature love of infancy and childhood, with its narcissistic overtones, may linger on into adolescence and adulthood, trailing behind it tentacles of selfish need. One may feel or reveal love mainly to gain something for oneself.

However, growth toward Christ-like love must move beyond this narcissistic phase. We must ask for a graced love that flows out toward the other for his or her own sake. Love means not only receiving from another's generosity but giving to others as the divinely beloved persons they are.

*Other-Centered Love*

The height of growth in other-centered love is reached when we recognize others and ourselves as the imperfect creatures we are while remaining utterly worthy of love in God's eyes. We are more than appears on the surface. We bear a mysterious mark of dignity no one can take from us, a mark we need to confirm continually in ourselves and others.

The lifelong maturation from self-centered to other-centered love is difficult, demanding constant effort and attention. So entrenched are we in pride, in narcissistic needs, that to come to such a chastening of love is impossible without the grace of God. At its most sublime heights love calls for our being present to God as the mysterious ground out of whom we and the other emerge. When daily concerns interfere with this Christ-like mode of loving, we try to remember that our chief call as committed Christians is to love others as God has loved us.

Forgetfulness of this call may cause our love to regress to the need-love of childhood. For example, tired from a tough day at work, a man may turn to his wife merely for relief of tension through an abrupt embrace. He may buy his friend a drink only to pour out his troubles, as if the friend had none of his own. Both examples are quite understandable at times. We have needs and expect others to relieve them. But if that is all love means to us, we may never move beyond childhood. To get relief and support becomes our main reason for loving. We find it difficult to refrain from imposing our needs arbitrarily on whoever will fulfill them. Love becomes a question of demand and supply, not an offer of respect and care. Other people are looked upon as objects to gratify our desires, not as persons infinitely worthwhile in themselves, independent of what they can or should do for us.

## The Celibate Dimension of Mature Love

Truly loving persons witness in practice to what we could call the "celibate" or non-imposing component of mature human love. Celibacy is not only a free relinquishing of genital sexual expression. It is an essential phase on the path to Christian maturity.

The dimension of celibate love, as lived by both single and married people, presupposes that one is centered in God who has loved us first. One then extends this love to others with attention and respect.

Understandably, all of us long to receive consolation from God and affection from others. Human love seeks reciprocity, but it does not need it at every moment from all people.

The summit of the celibate component of mature Christian love is its unconditional willingness to celebrate the sacred uniqueness of others and to love them whether or not they can alleviate our needs. In a phrase, we love others not for what they can do for us, but for who they are. Other-centered "celibate" love delights in promoting a person's well-being and in blessing his or her becoming. Consider how children thrive in an atmosphere where parents balance gentleness with the right amount and kind of firmness, where they are given room to grow and reprimanded when they overstep boundaries—all the while knowing through touch, tone of voice, and verbal communication that they are unconditionally loved by their parents insofar as this is humanly possible.

The average person could not maintain this self-giving

posture without finding some reciprocity at some time from those whom he or she loves. For parents, this may be the reward of a little drawing handed over with a warm hug from their first-grader; for spouses it may mean a gift of candy or flowers—even when there is nothing special to celebrate.

To mature in Christian love means to accept the risk that one may be asked to give love to others without receiving like love in return. One may have to go on loving in situations in which one finds less reciprocity than one yearns for as a normal human being.

### Witness to Divine Love

When these feelings of need seem most severe, we must turn our attention toward the always available reciprocity of divine love, even if this intimacy with the Beloved may only be experienced in the night of faith. The pain of loneliness can give way to the joy of solitude. The opening words of St. John of the Cross' *Spiritual Canticle* ask: "Where have you hidden, Beloved, and left me moaning?" At such moments we are given the grace to grow in intimacy with Christ, even in the midst of a desert experience. Sustained by faith, we become witnesses to the divine and the human dimension of celibate love. We create around us a climate of care to which others may readily respond.

The witness of celibate loving is rewarded when reciprocity is returned or granted as an unexpected gift. A student, client, or neighbor, usually indifferent to any show of concern, may express gratefulness for something we have done. A colleague may spontaneously compliment us. A client may say how much he or she likes us. We may meet family members or friends who are truly gracious to us. It is as if others sense that Christian love is responsive to the promptings of the Spirit and open in transcendent goodness to them, with no strings attached. Such love seeks no recompense in turn but gratefully acknowledges it when it comes. No matter what happens, we try not to betray or diminish our commitment to Christ and our service of others.

## Other-Centered Love Exemplified

An interesting illustration of unconditional love in a profession can be found in the work of good counselors or therapists. They form intimate trust relationships with many others without receiving always and necessarily love in return. They are ready to care for clients, even when there is no response or only a negative reaction from them over long periods of time. The celibate component of a good counselor's love consists in knowing and accepting the fact that he or she must care without demanding to receive like care from clients. One must meet them where they are in a loving way that transcends the frustration naturally felt when service only meets a wall of indifference or hostility. The best of us are tempted to turn back, but the power and depth of the celibate component of love prompts us to go on.

A counselor's love remains steadfast even when clients become aggressive, try to seduce the counselor, make fun of his or her questions, show jealousy toward other clients, demand exclusive attention, and only slowly gain sufficient confidence and stability to stop imposing their will on the world. This is a long process that could drain one's concern. Hence the unconditional love of a Christian therapist can only be explained from the point of view of its being an expression of celibate love rooted in respect for the essential nature of this client in God.

From this brief illustration, it may be clear that all forms of love in humanity can only approach perfection and be protected when at least a component of celibate love is present in them. Distinctively human loving makes possible the ongoing formation of the people of God. In the face of inertia and resistance we choose as mature Christians to love others unconditionally with a love that conforms as closely as possible to God's love for us.

Married love reaches its best expression when the celibate component has sufficiently matured. Single men and women find the value of their vocation immensely enhanced when they expand their capacity for celibate love to all people inclusively.

In both marriage and the single life, the celibate moment may be experienced intensely when we discover in each other an ultimate inner solitude that only the transforming presence of God can penetrate. In celibate concern we do what we can to foster in one another mutual transformation. We stand in awe before the unspeakable mystery of any person's brief life on earth. We choose to love and to go on loving until we pass over in silence to the bliss of eternity.

## Chapter XIII

## Living a Committed Single Life in the World

As a life style, committed Christian singleness expresses one's availability to manifest Christ's love in ways that transcend the exclusive obligations married persons have to their spouse and children. To be sure, this availability can be lived out in many ways. Some single people may be called to ministry among the homeless while others may become artists, scientists, manual laborers, entertainers, technicians, or teachers. As a symbol, singleness expresses the solitary fullness of intimacy with the Trinity to which all Christians, single or married, are ultimately called.

Commitment to the single life cannot be closed in upon itself. It calls for consecration to Christ within a state of life that temporarily or lastingly makes one available to his redemptive plan for humanity for all ages. On this plane there is no separation between Christian celibacy and Christian marriage. Marriage too is a calling of Christ and a commitment to one's family as members of Christ's body. Both Christian marriage and Christian singleness are providential forms of life in which men and women consecrate their humanity by the spirituality either of marriage or of celibacy.

The single life is one way to foster intimacy with Christ

and to participate in the salvific history of humanity and culture. It, as well as the married life, may become a meaningless burden, devoid of life-giving possibilities unless one's graced, formative commitment is periodically rekindled and renewed. If Christian celibacy lived in the world by laity does not lead to the gift of oneself to Christ and others in joyful surrender, it can breed the conditions for self-centered preoccupation or sensual indulgence.

Both Christian marriage and Christian singleness are forms of consecration in and through which the Lord himself is present in the church and in the world. Both callings as lived by lay Christians presuppose a special grace. Both have their joys and sorrows, limits and potentials.

We can only live these basic life forms as laity if we devote all that we are and do to this consecration. We must not allow ourselves to drift halfheartedly into marriage or the single life without thinking through and praying about what path we are taking. As lay members of the church, we must make a personal decision in this regard keeping with the directives of our faith tradition.

In Christianity, unlike in some other religious traditions, the experience of being summoned by God to marriage or the single life is viewed as a vocation to be responded to in a personal way. By contrast, in the past and in many cases today, in certain cultures that are not Christian, parents decided whom their children should marry. Personal choice was not an issue. Decisions were based on such circumstances as class distinction, the amount of a bridal dowry, the exchange of property, and so on. In some societies even today, elders may decide for traditional reasons that a son or daughter will not marry so that he or she can provide physical or financial assistance to aging parents.

Both Christian marriage and the Christian single life are expressions of love for the Risen Lord and his action within us. Maximum respect for uniqueness characterizes the Christian way of choosing to follow a call to marry or remain single. Lay members of the church decide freely to incarnate their love for God and humanity within one or the other of these fundamental forms of life.

## Single Life as Sign

Christian single persons can only be signs of God's love in the world if they remain humble in the face of their calling. A holier-than-thou attitude obstructs the channeling of God's love to others. It corrupts celibacy and renders it worthless in the eyes of God. It destroys the basic meaning of self-giving love lived in the light of Jesus' own commitment to the single life of a layperson in the world.

A true celibate calling enables one to be more abidingly present to all who need our care. In married life this outreach of love to others is somewhat restricted by the obligation to meet primary responsibilities to one's family. In single life the expression of love can extend itself more widely and embrace whoever is entrusted to one's care by God wherever this need occurs in the course of a day, a month, a year.

Magnanimous love energizes single men and women to engage in labors congenial to them for which they are truly competent. Lacking this vision and commitment, single life may become more of a burden than a basis for life. No matter how appreciative of the single life one's attitude may be, it does not free one from suffering. To conform to Christ means to conform to the cross. This suffering is less a matter of what one gives up than of what one takes up in Christ's name. Choosing to live as single lay persons following the call of Christ will necessarily allow for greater availability. This means in turn exposing oneself to the possibility of greater hurt and pain.

## Singleness and Spiritual Dedication

An increasing number of women and men commit themselves as single persons to work in developing countries or among the poor in their own neigborhoods. Like dedication is shown by single Christians who devote time and talent to expressing Christ's love in everyday ways in the workplace and in countless arenas of cultural participation. Trying to make the best of their academic, scientific, artistic, technological, administrative and religious gifts in myriad situations in service of the Spirit is their way of imitating Christ. Single Christians who strive to remain faithful to God's plan may be tempted not to pursue excellence, to maintain the status quo, to put their own interests and material needs above what is spiritually right and at times countercultural. On the other hand, they may unwittingly become a threat to others who would want to level their originality and dedication. For example, in an office setting a single secretary may stir hostility, jealousy and envy in other secretaries who take the easy way out, refuse to work overtime when necessary and base what they do solely on monetary compensation. How does one handle a person who wants to keep alive in whatever he or she does some spiritual inspiration, some sense of transforming the world into the house of God?

When single Christians experience this kind of resistance, they may grow discouraged. They may be inclined to forget what their commitment to Christ really entails. They may want to conform only to their environment to avoid being hurt or feeling lonely. Peer pressure may triumph over intimacy with the Lord. When they find themselves alone, laughed at, isolated from the "in" crowd, at odds with a society that does not welcome their efforts to witness to the value of another way, they may feel overwhelmed by the desire to escape it all. Even if the time is not right or the person they meet is wrong, they may jump at the chance to start a family of their own. To base a calling to marriage on a crisis of loneliness or despair is unwise and risky, to say the least.

## Questioning One's Calling

Still, one can understand why many Christians would ask themselves: "Why not ignore my call to the single life? Why not marry the first decent person I meet? Why should Christ want me to depend on him alone when I could be enjoying the personal intimate love of a spouse and children? Have I chosen the state of life meant for me, or is there another direction I ought to take?"

At such moments single persons sense the ambiguity of their calling—its open-endedness, its uncertainty. The desire to find clarity and solidity in a family of one's own can be overwhelming. At such times, under great pressure, some people may make a premature decision—one they may live to regret for a lifetime. They listen to their own fears and confused voices or to the pulsations of a secular culture. Silenced are the whispers of the Spirit.

Mentally, a woman may realize that she is idealizing marriage, wearing rose-colored glasses, reading into the imagined spouse her image of what he ought to be. Yet, emotionally, she cannot deny the deep, albeit momentary, attraction she feels for marriage, whether or not she is responding to her own calling.

To be sure, something similar may happen to married people. They are just as prone to idealize what it is like to be single. In moments of marital tension, when honeymoon bliss is behind them, a husband or wife may fantasize about the comforts and freedoms enjoyed by single friends and colleagues, little realizing that they are going through similar turmoil and confusion.

The truth is that both states of lay life enjoy benefits and attractions. As experience teaches, that is by no means the whole story. Both states share not only in the joy of the resurrection but in the sadness of Christ's lonely, crucified passion.

## *Place of Lay Associations*

Christian lay associations assume new relevance for committed single persons in the light of cultural challenges. Belonging to such groups enables members to support one another in their calling and to alleviate the loneliness of the single life by creating an atmosphere of mutual respect, kindness, and cordiality—a welcome contrast to tedious and sometimes troubled work situations. The members of such associations strive to show one another the compassion Jesus extended to all whom he met, healed, loved and forgave. Appreciation of one's single life is not sustained in an association where the atmosphere is cool, rigidly organized, stifling of creativity, or secretly envious and competitive.

Commitment to the single life implies a promise to uphold and facilitate others who share this vocation and belong to the support association. Members do what they can to create a warm, loving atmosphere, open to suggestions of improvement and the creative development of social and educational programs. The same promise of support for each person's calling inspires married members too. All commingle in respect. All contribute as best they can to the creation of a gracious climate of companionship.

## *Place of Spiritual Friendship in Single Life*

Single persons, like all human beings, need to experience the gift of warm, caring relationships. Since they have made the option to forego marital union for the sake of following

Christ in this special way, the source of their interpersonal intimacy has to lie in the grace and beauty of spiritual friendships with people of the same and the opposite sex. We can never force such gifted encounters, but if we remain open to grace, they may come into our lives when least expected as God's way of befriending us.

Such friendships evoke thanksgiving. As friends, we do not make arbitrary demands on one another, though we are comfortable asking for help when we need it. We are available to be with our friends for serious conversations and relaxing recreations. We are able to reflect openly about our vocation and appraise its direction. We respect one another's originality, create among us a climate freed from tactics of seduction or manipulation, and, above all, foster a quality of encounter that opens us to the Divine Other in whom we have our being.

Such befriending is not a cut-and-dried enterprise, but an ever present risk, challenging single friends to face honestly their strengths and weaknesses. We try to relate to one another in tenderness and trust, knowing that the Lord we both love stands patiently in forgiveness between us.

This faith is at the basis of every soul-friendship. Faith makes it possible for us to talk to one another and to God about our secret hopes and fears, our successes and failures. Together we can pray to the Spirit to guide our decision-making process and any actions that may follow. We trust that God will continue to befriend us as we have befriended one another.

Paradoxically, the solitude, so cherished by single persons, enables them to be more available to others in compassion and companionship. A capacity for togetherness emerges out of aloneness with God. The profound belief that each person is made in the image and form of God impels single persons to reverence this holy center of privacy, to do nothing to violate it. Others are cherished for their uniqueness before God, not solely for what they can do or be for us.

Many single persons happily find that, even without conspicuously seeking this gift, they are over the years blessed with a fine set of male and female friends, married and not married. Some of these friendships are deeper than others, lasting a lifetime. Often they are formed in the context of a shared profession where colleagues can offer one another a network of support.

In the context of spiritual friendship, it is clear that sexual expression means much more than a mere genital exchange. The single celibate man or woman accepts in Christ that the beauty of genital intimacy best belongs to the exclusive commitment of marital love. One of the great potentials of their calling resides in the possibility of living with the Lord as their center and witnessing to the wholeness of masculine and feminine expressions of sexuality in encounters that are warm and intimate without being reduced to "doing *it* or not doing *it*."

Single persons are and must be warm, vivacious, fully alive. They are not demeaned by empty sexual experiences with ultimately faceless and nameless others but wholly in touch with what it means to be male or female in Christ. Because they respect each other's integrity as persons, they can seek the joy of companionship without the empty loneliness of lust. To be a real friend means to treat the other always as a unique subject, not as an object of self-gratification. This kind of treatment is sustained by mutual presence to the Transcendent. Just as Jesus blesses us in our struggles to be faithful to our promises, so we are called to bless one another. Just as Jesus wills our total good, so must we will the entire good of the friends he gives to us. By thus serving the best interests of one another, single friends stand in the culture as reminders of the aspirations all persons experience, even if they are unable to express them.

## Integration of the Single Life

The single Christian life strives, therefore, to disclose divine generosity in a wounded world. It does not matter whether one is a nurse, machinist, teacher, administrator, cook, artist, dancer or author. Every field implies some routine aspects that in and by themselves may seem meaningless from the viewpoint of our mission to share in Christ's transformation of the world. However, to live in the ebb and flow of recollection and action means to gather ourselves together from time to time in transforming solitude. These quiet times clarify our commitments as single Christians. The grace received at such moments enables us to serve more joyfully the children in our classroom, the patients under our care; to compose, dance, paint, write, study, compute, clean, and repair things better than we did before; to be more generous and gracious with visitors and people who come to complain to us, sometimes abrasively.

Recollected presence to Christ transforms the daily drudgery of isolated events to threads in an harmonious totality. Christian singles represent in a special style and intensity the receptivity every human being bears to the transcendent horizon of all that is. Human hearts, as St. Augustine said, are restless until they rest in God. All people are called to bind action and contemplation. However, this consonance stands in danger or neglect. For we live in a civilization where the sense of ego satisfaction outstrips the sense of human endeavor as pledged to the spiritual transformation of life and world. More than ever, committed Christians are needed who, by their very lives, participate in the transforming and redeeming plan of God for every creature on earth.

*Part Four*

*Living Community*

## Chapter XIV

## Living Community as Laity

Most people secretly long to be embraced by a caring community. Many of us have experienced the initial community of intimate family life. In some way, even if our families were far from perfect, we hope to replicate the warm sense we felt as children. Persons born into unsupportive, even abusive families try to make up for this depletion by finding acceptance in some group of caring people. In pursuit of this need, one is likely to encounter disappointment. A community of needy people may band together with the best of intentions, but no human group can fulfill unrealistic expectations. All too quickly cozy togetherness may degenerate into a pressure for emotional intimacy and communication that plays on needs for nurturing and over-dependency.

This type of community cannot attract and hold committed Christians in search of spiritual maturity. It may satisfy the wants of some members temporarily, but its unrealistic premise cannot be lasting. Thus one guideline for establishing an effective formation community seems to be its capacity to draw forth and uphold the spiritual aspirations of Christians seeking a more mature life in Christ.

What distinguishes Christian formation associations from more ephemeral groupings? What will almost guarantee a failed or failing community? A community is not a crowd.

Imagine a group of men and women who gather together on a regular basis to read reflectively, pray and meditate. Then picture another group of relative strangers marching to support a common cause. What binds the marchers together is not a desire for mutual formation in depth, but a temporary uplift caused by contagious excitement about a time-bound cause. Different from transient enthusiasm is inner growth over a long period of time by means of committed togetherness, supported by attentiveness to the deeper meanings of life.

The opposite of a crowd is a well organized collectivity. Take, for example, a platoon of marines. The platoon comes into basic training camp as a crowd of boisterous youngsters who in a relatively short period of time have to be transformed into an efficient fighting unit. This transformation can occur only with rigorous discipline, harsh training, submission to authority figures, and whatever else it takes to shape a crew of diverse people into a platoon that works all for one and one for all.

Too often Christians confuse community with a collective rigidity that molds rather than forms, that imposes rather than frees. The way in which certain special spiritualities impact on lay people has the earmarks of a collective style of training. A special style and emphasis in prayer, for example, is mandated as *the* way for all with little or no room for the integral expressions of one's own life commitments. No wonder that mature lay persons think twice before joining groups that demand the kind of allegiance and uniformity typical of a military unit. They do not object to the basic spirituality of the church as lived by one or the other group. They resent being forced to conform to this or that special expression linked with a religious or secular institute. Such groups are united by specific aims that a layperson may not necesarily share.

A fine woman we know, who had already been graced with an awakening to a more mature, committed Christianity, had begun to embark on an enlightened life of prayer. She decided to make a weekend retreat with a group devoted to fostering a monastic approach to "lay spirituality." The facilitators instructed retreatants in the use of the Divine Office and encouraged them to pray the Hours daily when they went home. The woman in question treasured this directive. She began the practice faithfully on Monday morning. She was, by the way, the mother of three small children, one still in diapers. The instructions she received held for the first two days, similar to what may happen when one starts enthusiastically a rigid diet. By the third day she was already beginning to feel guilty because she had to skip a few of the Hours to tend to the children. As a result she decided that perhaps she was not called to a deeper spiritual life after all.

This woman and her well-meaning mentors had in a sense violated the first rule of a sound spirituality: to begin where you are. The instructing monk who told her, a mother, to pray the Hours did not have to change diapers. Could he be faithful to the Divine Office if he had three small children to tend? Is it not likely that he would run into the same frustration? Maybe it would be better for her as a lay person to concentrate on the "spirituality of diaper changing." In short, she had confused certain practices of a spirituality developed in a special religious institute with prayer directives for all. The important thing was to deepen her prayer in the common ways offered by the church—in liturgy, devotions and prayerful reception of the sacraments—all the while increasing her love for God and her willingness to listen to the invitations of grace in the circumstances and events of her everyday life.

What are then the chief signs of a sound Christian community of committed laity? Interestingly enough, all begin with the letter *C* of *C*ommitment so they are easy to remember: *C*ongeniality, *C*ompatibility, *C*ompassion, *C*ourage, and *C*ompetence.

## Congeniality

The story earlier told is a good illustration of what happens when a person violates the first rule of congeniality. What was proposed to this mother as an essential ingredient of Christian commitment was not congenial with who she really was and to what she was called to be. Neither was it compatible with her situation nor compassionate in regard to her family. The word congeniality means more than being a happy-go-lucky sort of person, great to meet at a party. We can only be congenial with others if we are at home with ourselves and our own commitments. The word comes from *cum* or *con*, meaning with, and the same root from which we derive the word *genesis*, meaning the source of or the origin. Congeniality means to be at home with the basic personal way in which we are created in the form and likeness of God.

Lay Christians on the way to spiritual maturity are people who disclose and develop over a lifetime their original gifts in response to a wide variety of family situations, careers, friends and colleagues. When they come together in a Christian community, their aim is to confirm each one's personal commitment to Christ. Any threat by crowd or collectivity to level respect for one's personal calling repels them spontaneously. Neither can they be at ease when less mature Christians insist that the community imitate family life by providing the kind of parenting that fulfills emotional dependency needs. Respect for the congeniality factor also prevents one person's special spiritual enthusiasms or awakening experiences from being imposed on the group as a whole or on any of its more vulnerable members. This living out of one's congenial aspirations is modulated by the common spirituality of one's faith tradition as expressed in its basic prayers, devotions, sacraments, doctrines, scriptures and customs.

## Compatibility

Another characteristic of a Christian community on the way to maturity is compatibility. Returning to the example of the mother, she was given a directive that would prove to be incompatible with her immediate situation of being a full-time wife and parent. Saying the Divine Office daily would make it impossible for her to attend to the many responsibilities she also regarded as part of her marriage vows. Her husband and children might admire her efforts to practice a monastic spiritual exercise but, as she quickly found out, they would soon suffer in the process from her neglect of their needs. Sooner or later they would resent her piety and might in general be turned off by spirituality.

The word compatibility comes from the Latin, *cum* and *pati*, meaning to undergo with others the limits of a situation; to be subjected with others to the prevalent styles and customs of a locality or position; to endure patiently the frame of reference in which one finds oneself by virtue of one's calling.

Lay people must live their Christian commitment in an immense variety of subordinated styles, positions and professions. To be effective epiphanies of Christ in these settings, they must be compatible with the situations in which they find themselves. Their particular way of life in the world, while being congenial to their integral calling in Christ, must be compatible insofar as possible with the everyday sensitivities of those around them.

Imagine, for example, that a group of Christians, by virtue of their congeniality and compatibility, are committed to serving minorities. Compatibility for them may mean living in or near the neighborhoods where those who need their care the most congregate. In the same church another group serves society as corporate executives. Compatibility with their calling may mean behaving and dressing in ways that make others receptive to their Christian presence in the business community. It would be as pernicious for social workers to impose their style of service on executives as it would be for executives to insist that social workers dress and talk as they do. In the realm of compatibility, if a Christian formative community is to survive, there must be maximum freedom. Enabling this freedom is compassion.

## Compassion

Compassion, from its Latin roots, *cum* and *passio*, means to suffer empathically with our own and others' vulnerability. As bearers of Christ in the world we are called to show compassion for all people—family members and friends, rich and poor, those who share our faith tradition and those who adhere to other belief systems. It is a question not only of being compassionate with people in general but of showing genuine compassion in specific situations with suffering persons.

We may spontaneously manifest compassion for the vulnerability of a drug addict or an alcoholic. Without condoning the addict's actions or enabling the alcoholic to cover up his or her disease, we may empathize with their condition and perhaps reach out to help them concretely. By contrast, mocking girls who wear mini-skirts or secretaries who dye their hair or condemning people who belong to minorities or who practice other faiths would constitute a harsh and rash judgment on our part. Judgmentalism paralyzes Christian compassion. The more we come to know one another with our failings and vulnerabilities, the more we realize how profound our need is for understanding and forgiveness. It is not so difficult to bear with one another as long as we are in the first blush of initial community formation. In the honeymoon period of togetherness, there is less need for empathic compassion. However, the longer we meet and work together, the more we need compassion to hold the community together. It is the "glue" that binds a group. It teaches us to bear with and love one another. Such love is only possible through Jesus. He elevated the ideal of humanity to a new height by making compassion one of its central aspirations. Though he must have been tempted at times to give up in the face of resistance, he had the courage to continue.

## *Courage*

Courage prompts commitment of the heart to persevere in the formation of Christian community whatever the cost. Without courage it would be impossible to implement congeniality, compatibility, and compassion. Committed Christians may respect each other's uniqueness, respond well to the situation, and patiently bear with one another, but still they do not survive. Why? There are many reasons for their demise, including utopian enthusiasms that come and go, but one main reason has to do with the lack of courage to persevere when the honeymoon period is over—to continue in a determined way despite opposition from the outside or from within. Growth becomes more difficult when people try on top of this to respond to the demands of the times which they are called to transcend and transform.

Two reasons that may account for the survival of certain lay communities and associations, like the Salvation Army and the Red Cross, are the courage to persist in the essentials of their founding vision coupled with the determination to adapt this vision to the changing times. If members—in trying to preserve the essential vision—reduce it to one or the other work in which it was expressed, they are courting disaster. By the same token, if they only swing with the trends and fashions of the times and never return to the founding vision, they are likely to be swept away by history.

A special courage is needed to be open also to minor themes in the vision of founders, even if such aspects are not in tune with what the majority of the members or a lobby of them want to promote. For example, an association of lay Christians may have been founded to help people in underdeveloped countries. This ideal might mean addressing the immediate needs to provide elementary education for children, jobs for the unemployed, and food for the hungry. Later in history, when the country begins to develop its higher schools, its economic base, and its agriculture, does this mean that the founding community should die or might its original vision have included, at least implicitly, an opening to all people in need? Though a significant number in the country in question are now educated, employed, and fed, new needs in the spiritual realm will have emerged and the community can be responsive to these. When the needs of a rising class of professionals are not met, not only they but all members suffer from an uninformed or underformed spiritual consciousness in the country's leaders. The once oppressed may then become the oppressors.

*Competence*

The communal disposition of competence implies that each member strives to excel in the gifts and talents he or she has been given. It is not only at home but also in places of work and recreation that lay people are called to transform the world into the house of God. Competence and the pursuit of Christian excellence counter the lingering heresy that technical, material and functional, artistic and athletic involvement is less spiritual than other-worldly, pietistic concerns and practices. True Christian spirituality and the formation communities that uphold it by virtue of their Christ-likeness are incarnational through and through. This means that they do not depreciate the competence aspect of their practical commitments but penetrate it by inspiration and dedication to the Lord.

Nobody would be edified or safe if a fighter pilot, attempting to land on an aircraft carrier in the middle of the ocean, were lost in contemplation instead of concentrating on a precision landing. Similarly, entire plane loads of people would be endangered if airline mechanics, at the moment when they are readying a jet for take-off, were engaged in discussions about the life of prayer.

Absurd as these examples may be, they illustrate what a split between the spiritual life and everyday competency would be like. Mature Christian communities must overcome this split. Animators and members must help one another to realize how the pursuit of competence and professional excellence grows out of a life of commitment and fosters maturation. It is our firm conviction that the height of spirituality enhances functionality and in no way detracts from productivity.

## Chapter XV

# Forming Community in the Holy Spirit

A true Christian community is a mystery. No human effort can create it without assistance of the Spirit. A threat to the formation of Christian community is an uncritical implementation of the results of experiments in group formation isolated from openness to the Spirit. Without the Spirit's inspiration we can never generate a formation community in the Christian sense. Human sciences alone cannot account for its existence and continuation.

We need to go beyond secular efforts without neglecting their compatible insights. Only a community of Christian formation that relies also on the power of the Holy Spirit can become a "pneumatic" community, as distinguished from a merely "humanistic" community. The latter is explainable in terms of human inventiveness and the sciences that expound and sustain it. Excellent as it is, a secular community cannot satisfy the deepest longings of the human heart. Inspired aspirations transcend all that group dynamics, sensitivity training, encounter techniques and the psychology of human relationships can teach us. A pneumatic community emerges from a different ground. While it does not exclude the underpinnings suggested by these techniques and studies, it is rooted in a deeper mystery.

The pneumatic community nourishes us before we mentally know what is going on in our graced togetherness. A true community of Christian formation is called forth by the Spirit and taken up into a wider divine community beyond our boldest dreams, the community of the Mystical Body of Christ. No human effort can pretend to build this Body. We can only express awe and gratefulness for the ecclesial communion in which we already live as companions in faith.

Compared to this ecclesial community, any humanistic community is but a shadow. There have been many attempts to foster such communities, under the guise of making people feel good. What sometimes seemed lost in a morass of feelings was the respect due to each person's call and commitment. Mutual reverence degenerated at times into a sharing of raw emotions only.

In a merely humanistic community, differences in taste, style, judgment and talent may lead to collisions between members that are difficult to overcome. A deeper motivation to go on loving—even when the affinity factor is not present—is needed. From whence does this motivation come?

## Marks of a Christian Formation Community

To be sure, in Christian communities of formation similar difficulties arise. It is impossible in any human gathering to feel at home with everyone. Clashes are unavoidable. The question is: What do we do when they occur? A mark of Christian community is the Spirit-inspired capacity to surpass personality differences and to overcome human antipathies. In his Epistle to the Galatians, St. Paul preaches to the newly baptized that no matter their rank or status, whether they are slave or free, male or female, rich or poor, they are liberated by Christ (cf Gal 3:28). The deepest affinity of Christian souls does not reside in a kindred collection of tastes, qualities and styles of life but in a bonding that comes from being graced by Christ through baptism.

Instead of striving to outdo one another in competitive efforts, Christians are called to complement one another by their different contributions to the well-being of the community. In diversity they find strength. For example, one member of a Christian formation community may be blessed with more reflective powers, another with practical aptitudes. Together they contribute in different ways to the group. Still another member, who is neither intellectual nor practical, may be given the charism of a delightful sense of humor, and, after all, every community needs a clown! The Holy Spirit uses his or her talent to grace the group with a sense of laughter, relaxation, and light-heartedness. By the same token, those aesthetically inclined and talented will enrich the community with their taste for beauty.

People in a pneumatic community expect that the Holy Spirit will help members contribute to the common good in a variety of ways. They are ready to celebrate together in loving appreciation a wide diversity of gifts, no matter how humble and hidden these may be initially.

The Christian communities founded by Jean Vanier for the mentally handicapped are examples of pneumatic bonding. These special people, who are deeply loved by God, celebrate one another's dignity. God gifts them in their own way. Their holiness is often outstanding, even if their wholeness by human standards may be severely wounded. Christians like Vanier see the inner radiance of the handicapped. They care for these little ones as beloved equals in the sight of God. They are remarkable witnesses to the importance of appreciating in each human being the limited talents given to them by the Mystery. Their calling, as they see it, is to assist these special people to make the best of their abilities and to enable them to contribute in their own way to the human community. Their vulnerability is a reminder to everyone of how much all of us need divine protection. Those who work in the Vanier communities for a period of time marvel at how much they have learned from these simple people.

Returning for a moment to the topic of the humanistic community, we see that it is made up of the following components: socio-historical, vital, functional, and transcendent. All members, for example, have been formed in their outlook on life by social situations in family, neighborhood, school and career. It goes without saying that the members may come from radically different backgrounds, leading to tensions in their relationships. Differences in vital temperament are also obvious. Some are fast and abrupt, others slow and plodding. Likewise the functional way of organizing practical details may be as diverse as the membership. Finally, in their spiritual make-up, convictions and commitments, people may differ considerably.

All of these differences can fuel the fire of contention. They can influence the dynamics of community life and lead to irreconcilable disagreements, to open or hidden conflicts and subtle impositions that may deteriorate into painful contests. Of course, a Christian community is made up of the same components and hence subject to similar tensions. Spirits other than the Holy Spirit can be let loose and play upon pride, envy, jealousy, judgmentalism, greed, and addiction to power. These "bad spirits" lead to the same tensions experienced in any grouping of human beings. Christian community members try, however, in the light of their baptism, strengthened by the Holy Spirit and by church teachings and traditions, to purify and transcend the natural obstacles any human community has to face.

The pneumatic community is deeply grounded in God's grace and in a living Revelation. Both originate in Christ and his word. Through grace received by baptism and restored or deepened by the sacraments, we are already a community called together in and by Christ to foster each other's spiritual maturation. Every particular Christian community grows by meditating on his word. Because each graced grouping is a special expression of the Body of Christ, we grow together in likeness to what we most deeply share: membership in God's family by adoption. What binds us together as a Christian community is not a human affinity only but an affinity of grace, an ultimate call to divinization by participation in the life of the Trinity.

## *Manifestations of Graced Community*

This grace manifests itself in the Christian community under the following three aspects. First of all, as lay Christians gathered in the name of the Lord, we strive to appreciate not only our differences but also our hidden likeness in the Mystery of transforming love. We are alike insofar as we are gifted with the Christ-form of life. He is the innermost reality we share.

The second aspect of our graced affinity as community members resides in our complementarity in the Spirit. Each of us is called to be a unique Christ-form while serving the common good in a relaxed way that is compatible and compassionate, committed and creative. Fidelity to this divine invitation to celebrate the gifts of all helps us to temper any excessive manifestation of our own successes that might unnecessarily irritate or discourage other members. The Holy Spirit inspires each individual to practice a kind of asceticism in the communication of his or her own attainments and talents. Compassionate respect for the vulnerability of others must always prevail. The fruit of this sacrifice, when it is lived by all the members, results in a mutual confirmation of their graced affinity. No one would ever think of "lording it over" another.

A third outflow of our faith in the affinity of grace is a

shared openness to the inspiration of the Holy Spirit. The Comforter is ready to inspire any Christian community, whatever its charism. The Spirit directs it toward the particular aims and goals God wants it to achieve in the Body of Christ. A Vanier community, for example, serves the handicapped. Another grouping in the same city may serve the Christian formation of professionals. Obedience to our common inspiration, rooted in the grace granted by baptism, leads in turn to an affinity of sharing in the same purpose. For example, in an association devoted to the formation of Christian professionals, the members' shared concern for Christianizing their commitments at home and work will draw them closer together and strengthen their original aspirations.

A community can lose its awareness of mystery and ministry and be reduced to a kind of service association. Many groups that start out with high ideals break up because they do not realize in time the signs of deterioration. Gradually they slip away from the life of prayer and place more and more emphasis upon functional methods, means and results. In their eagerness to expand their labors of love, they spare less time for spiritual reading, meditation, prayer, and sacramental life.

Leaving no room for abiding with the Spirit, their attunement to pneumatic inspiration begins to erode. They become alienated from the holy ground that nurtures their purpose of existence. They rely before they know it on human cleverness and measurable methods of plotting the success of their ministry. If in the course of time their success and status would begin to diminish, they have nothing substantial to fall back upon. Soon the community they started with such hope begins to crumble as they sink into a kind of low-grade communal depression. Paradoxically, the Holy Spirit may use such a moment of crisis to reawaken the members to the central importance of prayer and to the priority of restoring time and again, with God's grace, their initial inspiration.

# Part Five

# *Commitment and Human Work*

## Chapter XVI

## Work Consciousness in Christian Laity

In the life of Christian laity, one can detect a rift between labor and religious experience, between commitment to work and to God. This "split" may be more readily understood if we sketch the history in which Christian lay consciousness was formed.

If we could return in time to approximately the seventh century, we would witness a Christianity marked by a unifying vision of leisure and labor, faith and work. Life as a whole was beheld as a divine appeal, a holy service of the Most High. Dedication to plowing, seeding and harvesting was not experienced as abandoning the sacred for something profane, but as a consecrated endeavor aimed at securing nourishment for the people of God. The work of spirited defense of hearth and home was not perceived as a worldly adventure split off from faith but as a sacred obligation toward God's chosen people. Political and administrative functions alike were integrated within religious consciousness.

Understood within the framework of this consciousness, production and participation in community projects were not alien to religion. The work of cultivation, protection and celebration of this world by all social groups was lived as a liturgy.

Faith and work formed a natural unity, expressed in the phrase, *Ora et Labora:* Pray and Work.

## Change in the Mode and Meaning of Labor

By the end of the tenth century, the economic development of the west took an unexpected turn. Western Europe, finally freed from plunderings, pillages and massacres by Vikings, Saracens and Huns, experienced a sharp increase in population. Many formerly self-sufficient domains were no longer capable of caring for their people. An increasing number of peasant serfs were forced to send their sons into the world to work outside their domains. Serfs had to fulfill obligations to their lords by relinquishing part of their harvest. For children who could not survive by working on the farms of their parents, three possibilities were open.

One was to live on the charity of church and society as vagrants, beggars or itinerant laborers. The second was to look for wasteland outside the domain and farm it as independent tenants for an owner. This second option led to the emergence of a new type of work community, the village, a society of poor peasants who were no longer protected by a knight. The third possibility was to enter the economy of trading.

Trade began simply. In some areas there was an abundance of products that could not be consumed by the local population. Merchants sold them in regions where the same was scarce. Increasing populations led to a rapid increase in commercial labor. Merchants settled down as free burghers in cities, finding favorable locations at roadways and harbors. Craftsmen and artisans were also drawn to the cities. Their work served the needs of the burghers, while the labor of the peasants in villages took care of their food supply.

New economic relations were incorporated in work organizations called guilds. Money became the most important medium of exchange. Initially the guilds tried to link labor and religion. Gradually this inner integration was expressed externally in processions and pageants, still seen in parts of Europe today.

To be sure, this new situation changed forever the sense of an agrarian society. The economic self-sufficiency of former domains was broken apart by the commercial labor of free farmers and merchants. Due to increasing competition, conflicts were unavoidable. They changed our western appreciation of the very meaning of work. They foreshadowed the ambiguity still felt by Christian lay laborers today.

## *Work with Money To Make Money*

Up to this time, trade was necessary only when the population of a domain was threatened by a bad harvest, crop failure or natural disaster. Trade was then utilized as a kind of primitive Red Cross operation, a social emergency service. Representatives of other domains traded what crops they could spare with a stricken population. In return they asked only for what people could reasonably give or promise to give back.

Money at the end of the tenth century was not productive per se; it was kept for use only for life's necessities and for security in time of disaster. Money was thus also an emergency treasury to be lent to those who needed it to survive. Social consciousness revolted against any person who dared to ask interest for this kind of aid, who tried to profit from starvation and misery. It seemed against Christian conscience to enrich oneself by trading for extra profit or by the labor of money lending. To do so was in direct opposition to the central tenet of love of neighbor to which the former styles of labor were related, at least implicitly.

Burghers who made the work of trading or of money lending their means of livelihood could deny but not destroy their conscience. Their conscience was still formed in response to the demands of the former style and meaning of labor. They began to feel, albeit vaguely and darkly, that the work of trading and money lending was irreligious, a necessary evil in which they unfortunately had to indulge to survive and prosper within the new labor structure of society.

What was happening in actuality was a conflict of conscience. European laity experienced for the first time a serious split between everyday commitment to new kinds of social labor and their commitment to the life of the Spirit.

In the former society not only economy but also the work of study, of justice and of law was permeated by the unity of labor and religion. New laws, established in service of the work of trading and money lending, were experienced as irreligious or even anti-religious by lay persons who nonetheless needed them to protect the work of commerce. Thus the disjunction between spiritual experience and daily labor gradually deepened. The new laws were experienced as merely mundane, having little or nothing to do with Divine Providence.

The work of trading and money lending led also to a collision between clergy and laity. Lay workers or burghers needed freedom of movement, of contract and of property, prerogatives unknown among serfs in the past. These conflicts brought laity into contact with kings and powerful vassals who were willing to grant them exemptions from certain laws in exchange for money. In this way leading laity, involved in commercial labor and money lending, maintained the support of the king. The king in turn used their financial contributions to hire mercenaries and civil servants to keep him independent. Kings were able to protect the work of trading and money lending to such an extent that they achieved in many cases absolute royal power. In the realm of commerce, the only way to gain freedom of labor was unfortunately to turn against the political and monetary interests of the clergy. This contributed to the feeling that one's actions were at odds with one's religious conscience. Laboring away during the weekdays, lay workers could repress the awareness of guilt. This repression paved the way for the explosions of guilt that would culminate centuries later in such ghastly waves of paranoid behavior as the burning of witches and the mutual massacre of Christian denominations.

By the year 1200 cities had grown to such an extent that everyone had to accept as inevitable the new patterns of lay labor. Its workers were a force to be reckoned with. Both nobility and clergy began to profit from the advantages of a thriving economy. The disjunction of a spiritual and a work consciousness in the laity, set in motion then, has not yet been totally resolved. It led to spiritual uneasiness among people whose work was split off from prayer and who were basically unaware of their being driven by secret feelings of guilt.

## Chapter XVII

## Faith and Work in the Western World

The new mass of lay Christians formed by the labor force of the burghers at the beginning of the thirteenth century experienced themselves as citizens of a world that seemed to be increasingly at odds with a wholistic vision of society. The split between faith and labor led many lay people to the mistaken notion that the clergy should be identified with the church itself, while they—the laity—belonged to the world of profane work. There was a kind of unwritten pact between the two worlds, according to which the profanely laboring laity would assist the church world of bishops and their numerous clergy and religious. This religious society would, in turn, help the secular laity by relieving their guilt feelings and sustaining their hopes for salvation.

On many other points, dissension between the two worlds seemed unavoidable, for both engaged in the politics of power. Leading laity proposed political and juridical moves to curb the influence of noblemen, bishops and abbots. In this way kings and burghers could gain power at the expense of the churches. The church retaliated by using its prerogative of excommunication. Around 1300, for example, half of Christianity was in one way or another excommunicated. This declaration was effective, to say the least, because lay Christians—plagued by guilt and anxiety—could not afford to be cut off from the sacraments. Thus the division widened between the clergy who seemed to possess the church exclusively and the laity who "owned the worlds of labor, commerce, law and science."

This split in Christian consciousness led to two forms of life in the west, two ways of making a living, the sacred and the profane. It led in turn to two kinds of study, the theological and the practical or scientific. As a result of this rupture, the dialogue between profane and sacred learning became more difficult. Secular learning was not sufficiently enlightened by revelation; religious learning was not sufficiently stimulated by the work of secular thinkers. Theology temporarily lost its momentum. Its scholarly exposition continued, but its felt relevance for the actual situations of many laboring people weakened considerably.

## *Death and Idle Work for Earthly Profit*

Gradually, labor in society became equated with living in an occasion of sin. Sin seemed difficult to avoid in the world of secular work for profane gain. Thus the prospect of damnation loomed gloomily before the eyes of many medieval people.

From the thirteenth century on, dread of death hovered over western humanity. Death was experienced not as a transition to new life but as an ordeal, signaling the advent of wrath. Books, plays, poems, sermons, sculptures, and paintings of the period clearly reveal the perception of death. The imagination of late medieval people was preoccupied with its gruesome effects: putrefaction, decay, foul stench, the wriggling of hideous worms in rotting flesh, the ghastly deformation of once radiant women and handsome kings, death as a grimacing skeleton mowing down with its scythe sinners of all classes and ages, lost in idle labors for earthly profit. These notions came alive like nightmares in sermons, prints and paintings depicting the dark side of late medieval life. The celebration of death as a condition for the resurrection of a humanity which had fulfilled its historical mission seemed far from the common mood in this time. This morbid imagination was reinforced by the toll taken by contagious diseases that depopulated urbanized society. The black death of 1346 alone destroyed one-third of the population of Europe.

The conflict of conscience, sharpened by preoccupation with death and damnation, became for many their main tie with the church. Only the church offered the means of grace that could liberate people from sin and relieve the guilt and anxiety that kept boiling up from passionate involvement in commercial and scientific labors. It was not necessarily the love of God nor an active life that bound many lay persons to sacraments, devotions, pilgrimages and indulgences. What bound a number of them was their conflict of conscience, their dread and burden of guilt.

This mentality led to a mercantile approach to reconciliation and the soothing of Christian conscience. Lay persons doing well in the secular world desired to trade the possessions they earned there for the spiritual possessions of religion. Grace was experienced by them as obtainable in quantities that were in direct proportion to the number of good works, sacramental receptions and donations they could do or make. Also their relation to God was less an encounter in love that permeated and elevated their daily labor. It was for many more like a progress chart that could be computed in terms of mortal and venial sins as well as of good works and pilgrimages. The spiritual life of some was reduced to a preoccupation with the lines of demarcation between types of sin. The Christian consciousness of a number of working laity developed a "marketing" orientation that attempted to reduce the infinite to the finite. It obscured the mysteries of faith by means of material imagination.

Some Christians became like bankers with shares in the stock market of salvation. They experienced the church as a kind of insurance company. They counted and counted: so many Masses before and after death, so many pilgrimages and indulgences to pay off for so many years of purgatory, so many donations to the church. The spiritual life became for some a race for transworldly security bonds. In the consciousness of many Christians, sacraments and indulgences were a kind of magic wand. Lay formation became automated. Dimmed or missing was the awareness of grace in the reception of the sacraments and the gaining of indulgences.

Repressed guilt and anxiety reached a boiling point. The imagination, flooded by anxiety, ran amuck. The demon of dread inside was projected outside. People began to see devils everywhere. The person who behaved in an unusual way was suspected of being possessed. The punishment of scapegoats relieved anxiety for a while. But soon new victims were needed, for guilt was like a tide that could not be stemmed.

By the beginning of the fourteenth century, witch trials had increased to an alarming rate. Western humanity experienced itself as a battlefield of demons who waged war for the possession of souls. The projection of the demon of guilt and anxiety on people who were old and ugly or who behaved strangely led to the witch burnings. Townspeople would gather and cheer the torturing of a woman believed to be possessed by an evil spirit. Witches were said to have made a pact with Satan which gave them the power to spread disease and pestilence, to inflict wounds, to destroy the harvest, to change themselves into animals roaming the countryside.

### Double Life of Worldly Work and Heavenly Piety

Other groups of profanely laboring laity, especially in cities and at the courts of the kings, tried to find a solution to the problem simply by living a double life. They developed a pietistic personality while in church, a sinful one while in the world of secular work and relationships. Unrestricted pietism and unrestricted sinfulness could be found in one and the same person. For example, the political labors of Louis XI of France (1462-1483) would include stealing, deceiving, and murdering without mercy to work out his projects of power. At the same time, he would spend hours praying in his private chapel. Certain groups of intellectual workers manifested this double personality in the realm of thought. They would think and write like pagans and sensualists, while praying like genuine devotees in church and chapel.

The reformation attempted to remedy some of the symptoms of this split. While it partly succeeded, it also partly failed, for it did not cure the split itself or the root cause of these symptoms. Neither did the counter-reformation solve the problem totally.

### Repression of the Awareness of the Split

Secular learning often repressed awareness of the split between work and spirituality. Similarly a number of theologians neglected initially key discoveries of secular learning. They dealt insufficiently with the question of how to integrate commitment to the life of the Spirit with commitment to one's secular life.

A cheap materialism, a technical outlook, a superficial scientism were among the defenses that secular learning erected against the mounting inner anxiety of those who lived on this side of the split. These barriers between the sacred and secular conscience cannot hold forever. When the tension becomes too great to bear in the modern world, we will not burn witches, yet we may incinerate ourselves in a nuclear holocaust that could destroy everything. What is needed is a dialogue aimed at restoring the unity of our commitments to work and to spirituality. This dialogue must take place on all levels of person and society. Secular and spiritual thinkers should face the dividing issues and seek the integration of work and spirituality as one of the cornerstones of the twenty-first century.

## Chapter XVIII

# Functionalism and Formative Commitment

The problems confronting committed Christians today are similar to those plaguing civilization in general at the end of this century. Ailments that seem peculiar to contemporary lay life are in fact common to life as such in the western world. One obstacle to commitment in the workplace and to the reconnecting of secular and spiritual concerns is functionalism.

Functionalism should not be confused with enlightened functioning no more than activism should be confused with right action. Functionalism, like all "isms," is the absolutizing of a partial truth, in this case that the main value in life is measurable success, mass production and achievement, even at the expense of personal relationships. The effectiveness, not the goodness, truth and beauty of things, persons, deeds and encounters, is what counts. The key questions in a functionalistic society are: Is my life productive? profitable? practically relevant? These criteria become for many the guidelines of life and living.

Most, if not all, committed Christians in the west have grown up in a "doing" environment. Social organizations, schools, clubs, associations—all follow the same pattern. They too are functionally organized around certain aims and works.

In many cases, what a group does becomes more important than who its members are. Productive functioning is all that really matters to the participants.

## History of Service

In former, less functionalistic ages, some small groups of Christians came together to pray and work under the guidance of spiritual leaders. They saw the functional dimension as servant, not master, of the transcendent unfolding of life and world. Working with others in the context of Christian commitment did not mean functional organization as such but spiritual presence through service. Such was the origin of the orders of knights and guilds that specialized in the pursuit of excellence among different craftsmen responsible for a country's social and economic well-being. Service remained initially a secondary functional purpose, subordinated to the inspiration of transcendent values. The secondary aim of their labor flowed organically and continuously from a life of faith.

Sadly, in some instances, the lay guilds and orders of knights became wholly service-oriented. Later in history these same enterprises grew into vast organizations. The masters of the guilds were gradually replaced by people specialized in the complexity of modern organization. Often lacking a personal touch and compelled by demands of productivity, they concentrated mainly on functioning efficiently. In due time the guilds were replaced by secular unions and management corporations, on the one hand, and by specific Christian organizations concerned with maintaining gospel values, on the other.

In both types of organizations the trend to functionalism crept forward. In many cases it became an unspoken principle that the first obligation a member had was to uphold the external effectiveness of the group as such, be it a factory or a church-related organization. In some settings to be a committed Christian implied the readiness to be inserted into any empty slot in the system. Efficiency became the norm, the implicit, silent criterion, of appraising one's Christian commitment.

## Dominance of Functionalism

When functionalism takes over to such a degree, it may lead to the conviction that the only meaning of life and education is to function well. However pertinent this aim, service can never be the exclusive meaning of Christian commitment.

The trend toward functionalism dominates western culture as a whole. All of us feel pushed and pulled to perform efficiently and effectively, no matter what suffers, from health to family life. We feel guilty when we are not doing something. To do is vastly more important than to be. Committed Christians are no exception to this pulsation. It permeates society. Many feel guilty when they are not recognizably useful, as, for instance, when they engage in play, aesthetic pursuits, study or prayer. It is not unusual to hear generous Christians, who already labor excessively, express the desire to take on more responsibility than anyone ought to bear physically or emotionally. Such excessive availability erodes commitment because it leaves no room for personal inspiration. Christian commitment is meant to be and to remain a manifestation of human and spiritual values, sustained by relaxation, play, formation, contemplation and the appreciation of aesthetic beauty.

## The Art of Play

When we play or celebrate, we move in a field of meaning that is at once real and imaginary, binding and releasing. While we may play a game as if our life depends on the outcome, we remain conscious of the *as if* quality of the play experience. We realize that the world of play is not the world of labor and obligation in which we have to earn a living.

Play and celebration liberate us from worry and preoccupation. At a festivity we feel as if we can break through the restrictions of daily duty. Having fun makes the world of play relaxed, free and exciting. Stress and tension are kept at a minimum.

In play, as lived by children, practical purpose is not an issue. Being present to the moment and enjoying it are what counts. Compulsion and pragmatism are the opposite of play and celebration.

Play has an interesting effect on time. In play, time paradoxically seems to stand still. Even within the limits of the game, we feel liberated from the pressures of useful time. Hours pass like minutes. We want to treasure the moment. We are not present to time in the same way when we labor. For some compulsive workers, by contrast, "time is money," and it should not be "wasted" on play.

If we are unable to leave behind our worries and preoccupations and simply waste time, we cannot play or celebrate. This inability constitutes a serious deficiency. It means that we cannot restore ourselves for daily commitment by carefree immersion in the timeless world of play.

## *Effects of Functionalism on the Threefold Path*

Though functionalism affects society at large, it has a particularly pernicious influence on living the threefold path of committed presence.

*Functionalism and Obedience.* Obedience implies listening to the call of God in the dynamism of daily events. It encourages openness to the whole of our situation. To the functionalistic mind, however, there should be only one aim of life—to be useful. This one-sided approach may become the norm of change and adaptation. In this case, obediential presence to the transcendent becomes at most an afterthought. In the forefront of every decision and action stands functional efficiency. Obedience is reduced to listening to the practical details of productive life alone. Listening is attuned to the organizational side of things. Our need to perform as speedily as possible a variety of tasks leaves little time to be concerned about the persons involved in accomplishing them. Functional, not spiritual commitment is what counts.

Pseudo-spiritual pragmatism may become a substitute for spiritual commitment. If, for example, a committed Christian is a teacher, the effectiveness of her existence may be judged by the way in which she plans her classes, keeps the schoolroom clean, disciplines her students, and gets her grades to the office on time. The worth of her personal life is measured by the success of her professional performance. It becomes more and more difficult to appreciate the value of a task like teaching when the profession itself is leveled by a functionalistic, bureaucratic outlook.

*Functionalism and Committed Love.* Chaste, non-violating love means that we respect our own and the other's integrity not only physically but also psychologically and spiritually. We venerate the mystery of each person's being, everyone's inalienable right to privacy and community in the Spirit.

Contrary to the respectful is the pragmatic outlook, which sees self and others mainly in terms of productivity. The life of Christ-centered commitment may be stifled in situations where production and profitableness are the highest wisdom. Marital love may be transformed under the impact of this trend into a pledge of mutual usefulness. Couples become more a working team than a community of love. Celibacy becomes mainly an effective means of being available for the performance of needed functions in society, without being encumbered by an exclusive familial relationship.

This is not to say that we should cease promoting practical endeavors that may benefit many. It is simply to remind us that none of these modes of service can be equated with the meaning of committed Christian love. Ideally, service and respect complement one another, but in a culture which overvalues the pragmatic, it is easy to violate a person's integrity by forcing our projects on them as the only solution to their problems. This forceful approach is but one symptom of functionalism's pernicious effect on commitment in the workplace.

*Functionalism and Poverty.* Poverty of spirit opens us to the wise enjoyment and use of things not only in their immediacy, but in their capacity to reveal the hidden, transcendent meaning of humanity and culture. Poverty nourishes our appreciation of the silent companions of daily life as gifts from God. These gifts include clothes and furniture, house and room, food and drink, books and tools—gifts materially poor people know how to appreciate while the affluent are inclined to take them for granted. Poverty of spirit lets us taste the goodness of the small and simple things of life, waiting patiently for our appreciation of them.

Once these things become dear to us, once we can handle them with grace and care, we may be able to use them to foster God's work and the welfare of others. We live in the spirit of poverty when we listen to music, bring our eyes to rest on the beauty of an artistic masterpiece, enjoy the graciousness of our bodily movements, quiet our souls in the silent stillness of prayer. Poverty implies the willingness to use things wisely and respectfully and thus to grow daily in appreciation of them as epiphanies of the Mystery.

Without such an approach, the essence of poverty may be reduced to a spartan form of pragmatism. The assumption that only the useful is worthwhile does not enhance aesthetic appreciation. Prayer, play and availability for human encounter are deemed useless. When we relax—when we do nothing in the deepest sense of the word—we feel guilty because we seem to be betraying standards of conduct that do not include "wasting time."

Even if we play, we feel we should be at work. Play itself becomes a matter of meeting a schedule. In other situations, we find ourselves making excuses for why we are sitting still, enjoying nature, reading, dancing or listening to music. We feel compelled to explain what we are doing. Poverty of spirit should free us for recollection and relaxation. It should be seen as the beginning of any possibility of play, true human togetherness, worship, prayer, or religious experience.

As we consider functionalism and other obstacles to committed Christian living in forthcoming chapters, it is necessary to go to the roots of these ailments and their overall deleterious effect on the workplace. If task orientation has taken over in an office or school, people may be appointed to leading positions solely on the basis of their effectiveness as administrators. Workers may fail to report sickness for fear that their chances of promotion will lessen. Having been indoctrinated in the myth of service, divorced from the transcendent, any thought of self is branded as selfishness. Even though one may suffer, the work has to go on. Such is the perversion of common sense in a collectivity, disguised as a community, that glorifies mere practicality despite its dehumanizing potential.

One crucial responsibility of parents is to make the early years of their children's lives more than a period of utilitarian training. The unconscious predisposition to build one's life on motives of measurable achievement should be faced squarely by parent, child and teacher. Even the question "What is the purpose of life?" may initially be a utilitarian question, especially if one's existence is centered on excessive attempts to forge ahead in a functionalistic society. Consequently, parents and other professionals must recognize that functionalism is a serious obstacle to committed Christian living.

# Chapter XIX

# The Deleterious Effect of Homogeneity on Lay Formation

We are children of a civilization entrenched in a gigantic process of mechanization and technical growth. Thinned out, emptied out, burnt out, we fail to nurture the ground from which spirituality springs. We have found ways of minutely systematizing not only the processes of manufacturing but also the effective use of time. To keep the machine of mass production running smoothly, manufacturers must divide their products into homogeneous pieces. For example, goods are packaged in the same wrapper, houses are modeled after standard plans, cars are made on an assembly line, fast food chains line every highway.

This principle of homogeneity—of managing the whole by dividing it into equal parts—enables producers to provide the goods society needs to sustain an expanding, affluent population, but what effect does it have on the lives of individual persons?

We have been inclined to apply the principle of homogeneity not only to the organization of time and production, but also to human life as such. This attempt profoundly hinders creative commitment. Principles that have proven to be successful in the manufacturing of goods and services, in the organization of staff units in hospitals or of grading papers in schools, may be applied randomly to human life with no thought given to the dehumanizing potential inherent in homogeneity. While a tree may be cut into equal sized pieces of wood to make a floor, one cannot so easily trim down a human being. While children may be trained to execute a set number of effective routines, they may be unable to rise above the homogenized collectivity to become self-reliant persons.

The pernicious consequences of this approach may not be felt until the homogeneity dominating people's lives is put into question. In the past, spiritual formation may have been seen as a matter of training people to think, feel and act in relatively similar ways. Now, however, we must be prepared to live our Christian commitments among persons who express a diversity of opinions and display many different talents. Whereas in the past personal responsibility could be absorbed by a tribe or collectivity, now we must become aware of our personal call to witness to Christ in every walk of life, in every task and position that is in tune with our background and personality. That is why lay formation is not meant to be merely a time of information gathering but also one of growth in wisdom and self-discovery.

Are we able to disclose, in faithfulness to our life call, what we can and cannot do, what we can and cannot bear, to find our own pace of achievement, to bless adversity as a potential adventure in growth? We should be able to distinguish an immature, emotional utterance from a truly wise, creative and prophetic insight. True personality unfolding is a movement away from the complacent comfort of common consciousness and toward a personal awareness of self and others as loved by God and called to loving service.

Homogeneity, like specialization, has its time and place. However, absorption by the homogeneity of common consciousness can retard our formation journey. This homogeneous trend may be one reason why some Christians never seek a personal, intimate, intensive life of presence to God. Such growth can never be piecemeal. It has to involve the whole person.

## Homogeneity and Alienation from Spiritual Experience

One of the reasons why we may be alienated from spiritual experience is that we tend to rest complacently in a common consciousness we did not appropriate and expand personally and creatively. The insidious process of alienation from experience begins when a child has to adapt to the functional society. Contemporary adaptation is in great measure a training in alienation from spontaneous awareness.

Spontaneous childhood may hardly be recognizable after ten or twelve years of adaptation to the "god" of homogeneity. Grown-up children have for the most part lost their creativity. A kind of dullness and emptiness has replaced spontaneity. Unprepared for personal living, children may attach themselves to an "in-group" and before long be welded to the common consciousness that sustains it.

## Homogeneity, Groupism and Self-Alienation

Belonging to a group may be one source of alienation from personal experience, especially if we are not aware of certain factors that may already incline us to live outside of ourselves. Along with homogeneous groupism comes the unfortunate fact of technical specialization and the acute development of abstractionism in the west. We place ourselves abstractly in an imaginative situation out of touch with reality and expect our problems to be solved. If we have not come home to ourselves, to our own bliss and truth, no real or imaginary place outside will satisfy us. We will always be searching for a better place, a more understanding person, a more exciting group. In the meantime life as a mystery to be lived may pass us by. We may reject an offer of genuine love because we are too busy or too absorbed in our own plans to see it.

Again adhering to a group can be helpful in many respects, but it may deflect further formation if we make it the center of our life. In an atmosphere of in-group flattery, weak persons become weaker. The forthright and honest may not be given the opportunity to witness for a deeper commitment. The solution is to grow beyond the group mentality as central. We must move toward Christ-centeredness in the deepest core of our being. One way we can do this is by meeting Christians on the road to maturity who have not only found themselves, but who have come to understand contemporary pressures and the obstacles they hold out to ongoing formation.

It is disconcerting to meet Christians who frankly confess that they have never had a religious experience. They simply appropriated pietistic devotions but neither touched nor were touched by deeper inspirations. Little wonder they need the excitement of an in-group. Yet how easily this wears off in the humdrum of daily living. Without a real confrontation in which we face ourselves before God, also outside the group, we may not be able to overcome this obstacle, for life will never be as smooth as we dreamed it would be. There are always imperfections in ourselves, in others, in the church, in western culture. We are at once amazed and embittered by them. If we really begin looking around us, we may discover that these imperfections are not only in our family or place of work; they are in all communities, religions and peoples, indeed, in the whole of humanity.

No amount of renewal will ever remove the fundamental greediness, hostility, aggression, disordered sensuality, envy and jealousy of people, Christian or not. Facing the reality of fallenness is a first step toward becoming aware of who we really are. Finally, we may come face to face with the great truth of the Christian faith—that without the experience of redemption there is no hope of being freed from this or any other obstacle.

The moment we feel united in this struggle with others is a moment of grace. This is the silent sense of kneeling humbly before the Lord, of resting in the blessed wonder that we are truly loved. We have been redeemed by Another, who asks only that we open ourselves to the forming mystery of salvation, the unmerited mercy of God. From this hallowed ground true commitment springs, but the road to it is seldom smooth.

# Chapter XX

# Specialization as Eroding Spiritual Unfolding

Alienation from committed living actually seems to be on the increase in the western world. Many people live in the dispersion of common consciousness, strangers to their own interiority, valued more for the positions they hold than for the persons they are. Recognition goes less to inward commitments than to outward appearances. This trend leads to still further self-alienation. One may have an important position and remain poor in personhood. Another may be an indigent laborer yet rich in strength of spirit.

What happens in a civilization where specialization becomes an exclusive criterion of worth, where one tends to reduce human life to positional titles, economic status, earned degrees? What happens when people are valued only according to their capacity for production and success? their use of specialized knowledge and skills?

If a civilization attempts to streamline everyone to fit only into a certain specialty, the end result may be human mediocrity. Employees may identify their worthwhileness as a whole with material gain, titles, corporate "perks." As soon as a colleague attains a more distinguished rank or promotion, others in the company may feel envious or jealous. Tangled webs of competition, not based on personal worth but on the attainment of special favors, spread anxiety at home and in the workplace. People start to fight to be assigned to positions not really suited to them. A vicious circle ensues. Without such promotions they lose their self-confidence; with them they risk losing their true identity and potential for commitment.

In a society where the idea of personal value is linked to advance in the profession in which one specializes, it is difficult to be who one uniquely is. To engage in endeavors where one is truly at ease may be looked upon as an unwillingness to fit into a pre-conceived mold. Even so-called "lesser" occupations lose their dignity. For example, a woman who cleans and cooks for a living may feel inferior because she is not a top chef. She may seek a seemingly more prestigious profession solely because she overestimates the happiness that this specialization may bring to her life.

If a man is a specialist in chemistry, he may teach high school courses by day, go to graduate school for further updating by night, and center all of his reading around books, magazines and articles devoted to this science. Temporarily, that may be unavoidable. But if restriction of mental and emotional formation becomes a lasting life style, he may do less and less reading in other subjects like poetry and fiction. Chemistry is at the epicenter of his attention. It begins to direct his whole mindset and outlook on life. Such a one-sided orientation unfolds only a narrow margin of his personality. By contrast, when our chemist listens to music or engages in good conversation, when he enjoys nature and prays silently, he becomes richer as a human being and has more to bring to his specialty because his profession is integrated within the whole of his life.

Specialization is only one side of life. It must not be

mistaken for in-depth commitment to life as a whole. One can be a learned psychologist and a child in spiritual living, a professor of literature and a freshman in human relationships, a doctor of medicine and a failure in love. This is not to deny the need for specialization, but only to remind us of its limitations. While specialized knowledge may respond well to certain needs, it does not offer committed laity the formation they also need to excel as whole persons well integrated by the art and discipline of spiritual living.

## Reaction to Specialization

The central hungers of Christian life cannot be satisfied by means of an existence lived exclusively in terms of some specialization or position. We must be able to contemplate and celebrate, to cultivate fun and friendship, to enjoy aesthetic beauty, above all to pursue wisdom. With wisdom we seek to discover the true values of life; with understanding we try to relate to others in a reverent manner; with dignity we distance ourselves from surface impressions to perceive the worth of people and things in God.

The pain of mere specialization may evoke a longing for spiritual wholeness. Many young people express a growing interest in prayer, contemplation and spiritual reading but when they try to express what they are feeling, they often cannot find people who are comfortable in communicating with them on a deeper level. They can talk about technical renewal and adaptation, about ethics and moral values, but not about spiritual experience and formative wisdom. This does not mean that specialization must be forsaken, only that it should be placed in its proper perspective. Its potentially pernicious effect on the life of the spirit should be taken into account.

## Effects of Specialization on the Threefold Path

Obedience, we recall, is our commitment to listen to the whole of reality, to read God's invitation in events, and to answer it wisely and courageously. Exclusive specialization makes this listening difficult. We may be tempted to think that a limited insight covers the whole of reality and miss a wider vision.

Respect for others is also diminished when we see them mainly in terms of one specialization. For example, a mathematician may tend to judge a child only in light of his or her competency in the field of algebra. A testing psychologist may categorize a teenager merely in terms of a measurable cluster of personality traits. Executives specialized in administration may not know what to do with less efficient people. Every specialization throws only one shade of light on a person. If we let it, it may blind us to other dimensions of his or her personality. We should always be able to transcend our specialty in growing respect for the sacred uniqueness of the other which no specialized knowledge can hope to penetrate.

Finally, to live in a spirit of poverty enables us to distance ourselves from the specialized, pragmatic meaning of things to behold their epiphanic essence. It makes us foster beauty in all things. By contrast, if a husband is committed primarily to the cost effectiveness of things, he may be tempted to say to his wife, "Why should we bother making our home look beautiful? Can't we use our income for more practical purposes?" He forgets that a beautiful home expresses and fosters our humanity; it brings out the spiritual essence of things. To sense this beauty and build upon it is to see beyond specialized pragmatic knowledge alone to the whole spectrum of nature and culture. It is to see contemplatively.

## Chapter XXI

## Cultural Obstacles to Commitment

Certain trends in western civilization seem detrimental to the ongoing formation of laity, especially in the workplace. In addition to functionalism, four stand out as particularly problematic. They are: rationalism, behaviorism, existentialism, and pietism.

*Rationalism*

As a life style, rationalism is the rigorous attempt to base one's entire life and every human encounter solely on insights that can be obtained by means of one facet of human reason, logical analytical intelligence. Consequently, we neglect the light shed on our formation field by such powers as intuitive reason, affection, faith, common sense, and tradition. We undervalue observation and perception, experience, emotion and sensitivity.

This one-sided approach to reality segregates various aspects of any given situation from the whole for the sake of analysis. While logic is an excellent tool, necessary for managing life, if taken alone it may cause us to lose touch with everyday reality. Logical ideas, concepts, rationales, and systems of thought have a way of becoming closed in upon themselves. Divorced from higher intuitive reason, they could have a deadening effect, repressive of creativity. Logic is one side of intelligence. It is not the sole factor in understanding persons and culture. Yet, historically, analytical reason has superseded intuitive powers.

As humanity became more subservient to the processes of production and consumption, rationalism invaded the day-to-day organization of every quarter of life, from assembly lines to space probes. Affection, emotion, religious experience, and aesthetic perception came to be regarded in some quarters as interruptions, as pleasant breaks, to prepare one for greater effectiveness in the processes of logical productivity.

Rationalism welded human life to technique. It was not only employed as a tool of industry; it became the guiding principle of many social institutions. Schools, hospitals, churches and religious associations, to mention only a few, were seen primarily as places to prepare people to assume their position in a task-oriented society.

Technical rationality is a great blessing. It becomes a curse when it is applied indiscriminately to all areas of life. This is what happened in western civilization. Humans became arms of machines. People began to live almost wholly on the plateau of functional rationality. Many lost the distinctively human sense of commitment of the heart to persons, causes and institutions.

## *Behaviorism*

A similar trend, closely related to technocratic rationalism and logical positivism, is behaviorism. No one would deny the human need to develop proper and effective patterns of external behavior. Conditioned learning or training is a necessary step toward personal growth. If you and I had to rely on our own insights to discover patterns of acceptable behavior, we would probably drive everyone around us slightly crazy. Long before we are able to challenge or change codes of conduct and comportment, we need first to adopt them without fully understanding their significance.

Behaviorism as a life style exalts conditioned learning—not freely chosen commitment—as the main principle of character formation. Life becomes a computation of rules and customs one never appropriates personally. Technical rationalism supports this tendency by training people to adhere inflexibly to the precisioned planning of life. The more smoothly one can be wedded to the machinery of a cultural or political system the better.

Christian communities emerge from the tumultuous seas of cultural formation traditions in which all of these forces are interacting. Mostly they do not question the value of technical rationality and the need for some behavioral training. But rationalism and behaviorism, when absolutized, soon stifle the spirit.

Even theology can become theological rationalism. One assumes conceptualization, traditional or progressive, will automatically guarantee mature Christian commitment. Nothing could be farther from the truth as half empty churches attest. One can be an excellent theologian and at the same time remain oblivious to the hunger for lived spirituality. One may be highly trained in theological abstraction and still out of touch with his or her inner self and the overall common sense needs of a situation. A clergyperson may specialize in scriptural exegesis and fail to realize that his or her sermon is falling on deaf ears. The dynamics of intellectual arrogance, of envy and jealousy, egocentric ambition and hidden pride, may operate side by side with displays of genuine piety.

To educate adult Christians in rational theology alone, no matter how traditional or progressive it may be, does not guarantee that they will address the concrete problems of parenting, working and witnessing to Christ in the community.

When the praiseworthy development of theological rationality is not complemented by a well-formed and formulated spirituality, many may be inclined to substitute theological propositions for committed Christlike presence to self and others. Abstract principles alone cannot help people cope with the unexpected crises life brings. Alienated from our deepest selves, we may turn the freedom of Christian formation into a rigid, well-reasoned but lifeless outline of do's and don'ts. Meanwhile, doubts, desires and passions grow unchecked in the depths of our interiority, exploding with volcanic power when least expected.

Theological formation ought to be complemented by formation in the spiritual life. Spirituality, as expounded in scripture, liturgy and the texts of classical and contemporary spiritual writers, has been sadly neglected in our times. The probings, recommendations and language of spirituality are deemed obsolete and out of touch with the psychological and social conditions of humanity.

Understandably, if spirituality is not updated in content and expression, it may appear to be irrelevant in the eyes of contemporary men and women. Often all they know of the treasures of spirituality are moralistic outlines of some of its main points, accompanied perhaps by explanations of the ways in which these insights paralleled certain theological systems. In the meantime the main task of spirituality, to integrate religious experience and insight with the passions, needs, emotions, desires and commitments of people in real life situations, becomes secondary to training them in rational explanations of belief, in systems of thought and behavior disconnected from lived spirituality.

Foundational Christian spirituality has been supplanted by logical outlines and abstract principles. It has been weakened by a trend toward religious behaviorism or the exact execution of external codes of conduct which seem to promise a perfect incarnation of holiness. Behavioristic training, as opposed to spiritual formation, proposes lists of rules and regulations which, if followed faithfully, will supposedly lead one to perfection.

To be sure, a certain amount of conditioned learning is necessary for human maturation in any direction. Such learning is as much a part of religious formation as it is of any other process. Behaviorism becomes one-sided, however, when training in externals is not complemented by growth in commitment to our calling by God and a growing awareness of our formative or deformative motives, desires, passions, needs and feelings. We should experience not only the general meaning of the behavioral patterns in which we are initiated early in our Christian life, but also of what they mean concretely for our personality with its unique make-up, calling and capacity for commitment.

## Existentialism

Another obstacle to Christian commitment is the selfish climate of contemporary culture. One source of "selfism" is a mood and mentality we could identify as "existentialistic." It suggests that we can find meaning in life by ourselves alone, that we do not have to take into account a calling of God that precedes our daily existing and the experiences it offers to us. This mentality tempts us to deny that we are called to make our experiences consonant with our unique form or essence already present in God's mind long before God created our existence.

Our interest here is not so much in the abstract philosophy of "existentialism." Few people today try to live directly by the tenets of philosophy. Most are seeking for direction in the popularized versions of the social sciences, especially psychology. Therefore, our dedication to the spiritual formation of lay Christians orients our concern toward the unacknowledged existentialistic assumptions that may permeate certain developmental and therapeutic psychologies and their popularizations among Christians. Such hidden assumptions are deemed "existentialistic" in contrast to the well-integrated, traditional, essential and existential presuppositions of classical Christian philosophies.

Existentialistic assumptions are communicated implicitly and usually unwittingly by teachers, writers, counselors, therapists, educators and the media. Especially influential are popular communications. They affect directly and indirectly the way in which people begin to think about such ideals of human development as self-esteem, self-assertion and self-actualization and such conditions for growth as individualization, self-help programs, positive thinking, wellness, archetypal dream analysis, and so on.

Such popular aims and ideas can be understood in many ways. Some of them could be compatible with the Christian tradition of spiritual formation. The usual connotation today, however, is existentialistic instead of truly existential in the traditional Christian sense of commitment to God, not merely to self, in the sense of an "existing" or "reaching out" toward the unique essence or form God has in mind for us from all eternity. Developmental expressions, as used by certain humanistic psychologists, seem to suggest that we should actualize ourselves by following only the spontaneous experiences that flow from our everyday existing in the world. They do not speak about our existential fidelity to a God-given life call, unique form or essence that pre-dates and transcends created existence. They seem to suggest that we should esteem ourselves for our own talents, efforts and success, independent of our divine calling.

Yet only this eternal calling is the real source of our dignity; it precedes the efforts and effects of our existing in this world. Such unrecognized existentialistic presuppositions may invade developmental psychologies too. People may come to believe that successful passage through psychological stages of development alone is capable of redeeming them from unhappiness and lack of effectiveness, from many defeats in human relationships.

According to existentialistic thinking, our created existence is not really created. It is thrown into this cosmos by a play of forces and must find in itself all that will foster human evolution to perfect wellness. Certain popularized humanistic psychologies, no matter how helpful they may be, are in many ways often tainted by unacknowledged existentialistic assumptions. So, too, are numerous self-help books and cassettes. Many well-intentioned Christians in search of spiritual formation are affected unwittingly by these through adult education and self-help programs, through psychological and transpersonal spiritualities, through pastoral counseling courses insufficiently critical of the assumptions of their sources.

Not only certain humanistic psychologies, personal and transpersonal, but also other human sciences and disciplines, such as educational theories of human development, sociologies, and anthropologies, may be affected by unacknowledged existentialistic presuppositions. All told, they have helped to initiate well meaning people into a subtle, sophisticated selfism. Any ultimate selfishness—no matter how transpersonal and spiritual it may sound, no matter how individual or shared with a group or with a deified humanity or cosmos—interferes with the spiritual maturation of genuinely committed Christians.

In relating existentialism to the threefold path, we can see that the obedience of committed Christians is diminished to the degree that they unwittingly assimilate the hidden existentialistic assumptions of many human arts and sciences. Scripture counsels a full obedience to God's will as the basis of life's formation. It is the will of God that we make our daily existence more and more consonant with the essence or life form God calls us to from eternity. To the degree that we make the everyday experiences of our created existence absolute, our spirit is less ready to disclose and implement in obedience the life call that precedes our concrete existence here and now.

Committed love, chastened of selfism, means that we love ourselves and others as unique forms or essences pre-formed splendidly in God's mind. We all know ourselves and others in the deformity of our fallen existence. Such glaring deformation makes it difficult for us to love ourselves and others for who we most deeply are. We cannot yet see what we are called to be when Christ fully liberates us from our deformation and restores us to the image or form of God in which we are created. Only when we can transcend the view of our concrete existence here and now and believe in our hidden form or essence can we love ourselves and others as gifts of the Eternal.

Poverty or simplicity and relaxed detachment of spirit are difficult to attain when the power, success, popularity, and pleasures of a fleeting existence are the only things in which we believe. All are passing. Hence a radical existentialism, as distinct from healthy concern for daily existence as the embodiment of our essence or founding form in God, leads ultimately to despair.

## *Pietism*

Pietism is the attempt to substitute for the affective dimension of spirituality a vague arrangement of shallow sentiments, often unrelated to the inner calling and the corresponding commitments of a person. Pious feelings are harmful or propitious only in relation to what they mean for us: How congenially are they in tune with our founding life form? How compatible are they with our commitments? How well or how little have we appropriated them?

Pietism becomes disintegrative when a desired collection of pious feelings are superimposed on our personality. These unassimilated feelings may be at odds with hidden strivings and emotions. They may even be used as an escape from the painful task of facing reality or as a defense against graced transformation on a deeper level.

True spirituality, by contrast, cultivates a profound but peaceful self-confrontation in the light of the Spirit. Deepening presence prevents the pretense that we possess religious feelings described by others when in reality we do not, or at least not yet, experience them in depth. If we deceive ourselves about this grace, devotional sentiments may become like items we collect and add to an already amassed repertoire of rational systems and behavioristic techniques. All of these may lessen the possibility of deeper spiritual growth while enhancing a superimposed piety.

Rationalistic, behavioristic, existentialistic, and pietistic training may replace foundational spiritual formation. When this happens, many well-meaning Christians may seek and seemingly find intriguing ideas, exciting experiences, and clever systems of human development without increasing their readiness and receptivity for graced transformation.

Alienation from our real thoughts, motivations and affections prevents us from participating in the workplace as genuine witnesses to Christ. We cannot expect to grow in love for God and neighbor if we cannot wait upon the initiatives of grace. Sanctimonious sentiments, unsustained by graced inspirations, are likely to fail us in crisis situations and desert moments.

Accepting the limits of life is entering the reign of grace. Under the impact of rationalism, behaviorism, existentialism, and pietism, it becomes tempting to keep our attention confined in the opposite direction, that is to say, away from our need for redemption and toward self-initiated projects of salvation, destined in the end to fail.

## Chapter XXII

## Laity in the Workplace

Whatever our profession—teaching, law, nursing, medicine, social work, manual labor, sales, secretarial—or whatever our position—director, researcher, administrative assistant, tour guide, clerk—we have to deal with the challenge of remaining committed and socially present despite mounting pressures to perform well, to be impressive, to pursue success. We are taught early in life to shun the specter of failure, always to try harder. A competitive spirit, a clever tongue, an analytical mind—these qualities place a person in the winner's circle in today's world. How, then, can a sense of Christian service and the pursuit of excellence be restored? How can we disclose a spiritual meaning in the professionalism of any competent laborer?

Professionals, spiritually speaking, should be persons who literally "profess" through their work a sense of self-worth in Christ and a benevolent dedication to the community and the world at large. Doing what we do should be congenial with our call to express in our professional commitments who we are as images of God. Our work should manifest a loving compatibility with the current situation in which we serve the community. To the degree that we are dedicated, we shall find many occasions in which to exercise compassion for our own and others' vulnerable condition. These three dispositions—

transcendent *congeniality, compatibility,* and *compassion,* together with *competence, courage,* and *commitment*—are the formation ideals that laity should try to bring to life in the workplace.

Christian social presence at work aims to transform for the better our own and others' daily experience in and through service. Christian professionals, like others with whom they labor, feel swayed at times by cultural pressures, impulsive reactions, undue arrogance, and selfish ambition. They try not to succumb to these stirrings to the detriment of higher hopes and ideals. Vital energies and functional talents are placed at the service of transcendent attitudes and actions.

## Dedication in the Workplace

To the degree that the above process of spiritual transformation occurs, there need be no split between who one is in Christ and what one does. Christians ought to radiate outwardly the spiritual values they strive to keep alive inwardly. Such caring presence shines through their appearance and performance. People sense an integration between the heart of a Christian professional and the extension of his or her willing, deciding, loving actions in consulting offices, hospitals, law firms, research centers, mills, shops, or wherever. It is not unusual to hear people say: "Your heart is really in your work, isn't it?"

Formative Christian presence is not something tucked away inside one's heart; it has the potential to radiate outward in a helpful, possibly inspiring, manner through our relaxed yet skillful, our playful yet dedicated professional life. This is why others remember: "It is not so much what you said or did so skillfully but the way you were. That meant more to me than words can contain, and I'll always be grateful to you."

The maintenance of committed Christian presence in the workplace involves a lifelong effort. In the deepest sense what sustains this presence is our abandonment to the beneficial meaning of the Formation Mystery in faith, hope and love. No matter what happens to us in our here and now situation, we are inclined to seek the meaning of each event within the context of the Mystery undergirding and embracing all persons, places and things. It is this attitude of abandonment that enables us to keep growing in the life of the Spirit in and through our everyday labors. The spirituality of work sustains our loving service of others despite discouragement, failure and disappointment.

Each time we surrender in faith to the providential meaning of a routine event or unplanned surprise in our working day, we prevent the erosion of Christian presence and its potential depletion. Though we may not always be able to see the light at the end of the tunnel, we wager that something ultimately good is happening and that in due course we shall understand its meaning more fully. We trust that Someone bigger than we are will carry us through, no matter what happens.

## *Depletion Process in the Workplace*

Lacking these qualities of Christian presence, laity in the workplace run the risk of "burning out." How does this crisis occur? It begins with an initial phase of exalted aspirations and ambitions. Recall your first job. You were going to set the world on fire. Such enthusiasm is important because it symbolizes our good will to make the world a better place, to help people become happier, to bring more consonance into otherwise dissonant situations. Enthusiasm of this sort is good. What causes trouble is the exalted nature of our intentions insofar as these are rooted less in realistic appraisal of the situation and more in our egocentric pride-form or in a romantic notion of Christian service.

Note the language characteristic of these obstacles: "*I* want to cure the ills of the world. *I* want to resolve the blatant issues of social injustice. *I* want people to shake themselves out of this torpor of complacency, now!" These words manifest too much trust in our own power and enthusiasm, too little reliance on the Holy Spirit.

Next comes a phase of recurrent, yet still widely spaced apprehensions of dissonance between our exalted aspirations of what should be and a more realistic approach to what is and can be done on basis of available functional skills, physical stamina and the limitations of the work environment. In short, we discover that things are not working as we had hoped they would. On the one hand, we retain our dreams while, on the other hand, we see them dashed against the harsh buttress of reality.

## *Marks of a Christian Presence Crisis*

Things move rapidly now toward the erosion phase. Apprehensions of dissonance ("Something is radically wrong . . .") increase. We sense intuitively that all is not well while not knowing exactly why. But our work intentions are so good! Along with an increased sense of uneasiness comes a more noticeable diminishment of our Christian presence.

It unfolds in two alternating stages. The first is marked by a temporary but real depletion of energy, interest, altruism and other aspirations to witness to Christ in the workplace. For instance, we may find it harder and harder to get out of bed and begin the day. We wonder what we are doing in this office or school or factory. No one seems to pay attention to our ideas or ideals.

A second mark of the crisis is that we fall back upon routine modes of conditioned social behavior. We look and act the part of the devoted teacher, physician, nurse, social worker, lawyer, secretary, ballet dancer, actor, minister, cab driver. We play our role well, but our heart is not in it. Hence the crisis: on the one hand, a depleted heart, and, on the other hand, a well-conditioned code of behavior, a willful keeping up of appearances.

What occurs next in the process is the dominance of this crisis to such a degree that we may feel lost and abandoned in meaningless processes of routinized labor, apparently unimportant for our growth in the Christ form of life. We may come to think of ourselves as miserable failures. How will we respond to such a state of doubt and spiritual depletion? In a negative or in a positive way?

## Negative and Positive Solutions

Negatively, the scenario runs like this. We become more or less indifferent: "They don't care about me, so why should I care about them. I'll do my job, draw my pay, and for the rest—let them take care of themselves." Typically, we experience an inertia that shows up in doing exactly what we have to do not to be fired, but no more. Such inertia is the opposite of the radiation of Christ-like concern and compassion, of the skillful dedication we, as Christian professionals, claim to "profess." Then, too, we opt to maintain rigidly the proper codes of behavior, mastering well the rubrics of the apparent form appropriate to our profession. But we develop simultaneously a dreadful strain between life after hours and the new begrudged time at work. This split is a sure sign of eroded Christian presence in the workplace.

There is a more positive solution to the crisis that can occur along with the restoration of new purpose and vitality.

This formative (versus deformative) response begins with the reaffirmation of an appreciative, hope-filled abandonment to the Formation Mystery in prayer and reflection. This kind of inner spiritual nourishment is essential if we are to nip depletion in the bud. It often helps to find a quiet place for rest and recollection, to step aside from the turmoil for a few days to regain our perspective. At times we do need to create space between ourselves and the workplace to see what is happening and to regain a more transcendent, realistic, less exalted view.

Transforming the world through work (the call of the laity) means doing the best we can within the limits of any given situation. This goal tempers illusions of perfectionism as well as the expectation that life will proceed according to our plans. To be abandoned to God is to remain open to surprises. Attitudes of surrender and realistic acceptance enable us to cope more effectively with the situation that evoked the crisis in the first place.

Effective coping means admitting candidly what we appreciate and what we resent, what we agree to live with and what we shall seek to improve. Rather than letting bad feelings fester, we try to find creative solutions that bring peace to our heart and foster peace in formerly tense situations. Though the crisis of erosion and depletion of Christian presence will repeat itself, if we treat it as a positive challenge, a true formation opportunity, we shall be that much closer to more lasting reformation and repletion.

## *Fostering Appreciation*

We may now ask if the positive solution, outlined previously, can become our characteristic way of being with God and others? To facilitate this movement, we would be wise to cultivate a firm yet gentle, critical yet creative, appraisal of our life direction in relation to our unique commitment, to other people and to the Formation Mystery enfolding cosmos and humanity.

The appraisal disposition inclines us to look for the spiritual significance of everything that happens to us. It implies a basic belief that there is a hidden providential meaning in all that transpires in our professional situation. If we are to maintain the abandonment option, it is necessary to open ourselves again and again to God in primordial faith, hope and love. Any withholding of these virtues leads inevitably to the discouragement, despair, and closure typical of eroded Christian presence.

Questions like these must be asked on a regular basis: "Who am I most deeply before the Mystery? How has the Mystery of hidden meaning directed my life of labor compatibly in this situation? In the light of this basic congeniality and compatibility, how can I learn to be more compassionate toward the vulnerability I detect in myself and others? What can I do competently?"

Finally, we must be comfortable with the tension that is always present between congeniality (the right and freedom to be who I am) and compatibility (the necessary limits of every human situation). Reformation of Christ-centered presence in the workplace requires that we learn to live compassionately with the inevitable pull between our limited life and the given, also limited, labor commitments within which it unfolds.

## Conditions Reforming and Facilitating Christian Presence

Other means of reforming social presence call for practical interventions that complement ongoing appraisal and facilitate reformation. The first deals with the basic question: "Should I partially or totally change my style or place of labor? Is there so much incompatibility between the limited, vulnerable me and the situation in which I find myself that I have to begin to initiate a partial or total change more in tune with my unique potential?"

This is not an easy question to ask, especially if people have been embedded in socially conditioned behavior and fear the insecurity implied in change. It may also be the case that prior commitments make it impossible for one to make a major change. In this instance it is essential that we at least be conscious of the problem and endure potentially depleting circumstances for higher motives—like providing for the care of our family.

At such junctures of life, we may benefit from some form of formation counseling, either in common or in private. Discovering or rediscovering the true direction of our life's commitments is essential if we are to experience peace and joy as laity in the workplace.

We may need to consider, of course, modifying either partially or totally our way of working. It is essential that we experience some commitment of heart, for where our heart is, there we shall be. Others will sense whether we are phony or sincere. It helps if we can be open humbly to their remarks about our performance. There is often a grain of truth present even in the unjust comments we hear about ourselves. Perhaps there is room for improvement in some areas. If we want to do a better job, we may have to modify some aspect of our approach, appearance or attitude. For example, is there something static about the way we relate to people, a kind of inflexibility that refuses to take into account the differences between us and our subordinates, colleagues, and superiors? Do we always expect others to bend to our ways? Do we insist on having the last word? Why do we demand that others change, never us? Are we afraid to widen our social circle for fear of losing control of easily managed dependency relationships?

It is wise to remember that we are not isolated professionals seeking autonomous power and positions of status. We are persons called by Christ and destined to care for one another, for the people we are committed to serve. Three main dispositions facilitating this aim in the workplace are: empathic appreciation, expressive communication and manifest joyousness.

*Empathic Appreciation.* This disposition enables us to co-experience, at least imaginatively, what others are going through. It is essential, for instance, in the health and service professions, in those of teaching, of buying and selling, in administration. This disposition also helps parents to relate to children. It says in effect that we accept others as they are, that we reverence their uniqueness, that we bless their being with us. Empathy means that we "feel into" what the other is feeling in a heart-to-heart moment. Others often blossom under the radiance of such an appreciative stance. They know that though a supervisor or teacher may need to pass practical judgments on their work, he or she appreciates their ultimate worthwhileness and creative potential.

Empathy enables us to appreciate what socially eroded people everywhere are going through. They are in college dormitories, in families, in decaying neighborhoods, in a variety of workplaces. We appreciate their plight; we try to help them to live it through because we have been there ourselves. Even if we have not gone through their actual experience, we can imagine what it is like, via analogies with our own. Such empathy not only enables us to help others through a social crisis; it also makes us more inclined to be compassionate toward ourselves when we get into a similar predicament.

*Expressive Communication.* How we express our appreciation depends on the given situation, but in general we need to be mindful of the need that others feel for sincere, open-hearted communication. Though many techniques of communication have been developed in our time, people still complain of not being listened to or understood. Frequent laments are heard, for instance, from hospital patients. They praise the quality of the health care they are receiving in one breath while reporting in the other poor communication between themselves and doctors and nurses. Verbal communication is important when one probes a patient's history, but so too is the nonverbal message of a gesture, a smile, a touch of hands. All of us probably have this capacity for expressive communication, but in many of us it remains underdeveloped.

*Manifest Joyousness.* A third disposition conducive to the restoration of Christian presence is joyousness. Joy, a transcendent attitude, may be distinguished from satisfaction on the functional level and pleasure or gratification on the vital level. Joy can be felt even when we do not experience much that is fulfilling functionally speaking or gratifying vitally. For this reason joy may only be explicable in the light of appreciative abandonment to the Formation Mystery as benevolent. Consider the joy that radiates from the face of Mother Teresa of Calcutta as she walks among destitute children and the dying. Neither injustice nor suffering, pain nor death, can shake the confidence of her smile. Her transcendent joy is spontaneous; it cannot be forced; it wells up from deep within her soul. It is present even when she must weep, for it is rooted in unshakable faith, hope and love.

By extension, responsive, joyous lay professionals become like a light on the mountain. They move through life like dancers in tune with the rhythms of contemplation and action, seeing the whole symphony of formation in cosmos and world, and doing what has to be done. Gracious, open, receptive, gentle, joyful—these dispositions create a buffer zone between us and the erosion and depletion process. The more such dispositions of the heart become second nature to us, the more will our professional and social presence radiate the goodness, truth, and beauty characteristic of lay Christian formation.

## Repletion Sessions

Due to the demands made upon laity in their social service and professional obligations, repletion becomes not a luxury for an elite few but a survival measure for all. We need renewal occasions that deal less with questions of outer change and more with the challenge of transformation from within. Altering the situation in which we find ourselves does not happen easily. What can be changed for the better are such inner Christlike attitudes as compassion, appreciation, empathy and joy.

Formative renewal sessions should be designed to help lay people get in touch with their experiences in the workplace so that they can better understand the phases of the erosion-depletion cycle in their life. Here persons deal with the core issues of self-formation in Christ, focusing during this brief respite on questions of spiritual congeniality and compatibility more than on projects promoting institutional change. The distinctive character of repletion sessions is that they help people develop the inner and, by extension, the outer conditions necessary to foster a more congenial, compatible, compassionate, and competent Christian presence. Persons conducting such sessions need to understand the nature of foundational human formation and its Christian articulation so that they can help participants overcome deformative exaltation tendencies, anxieties, insecurities and perfectionistic illusions, such as that of being totally available to people and responsible for solving all their problems.

Facilitators can also help professionals deal with the false guilt that emerges because they cannot do more. Such sessions relieve the burden of unhealthy guilt by bringing the causes of it to the fore. For instance, participants may be counseled to recognize the tyranny of obsessive ideas, such as their erroneous belief that relief of certain adverse economic conditions will in and by itself cause all injustice to cease. No outer reformation of unjust conditions will hold in the long run unless people are willing to undergo a profound inner change of heart. False deformative guilt may emerge, for instance, when well-meaning action groups do their best and still people in a certain region are no better off.

People need to see the difference between aspirations or wise ideals and the tyranny of absolutized reformation projects that demand instant action from all regardless of their talents, limits and vulnerabilities. Some people are called to serve in soup kitchens, others in research laboratories; some in their home countries, others in foreign cultures. To seduce anyone to betray his or her calling under the impact of false guilt is a mean and cruel act of social injustice.

With the help of repletion sessions, lay professionals can trace the causes of erosion and of the corresponding collapse of their spirituality. The process started with feelings of uselessness when projects failed; lack of trust when others disappointed them; waning of their sense of self-worth in Christ when they gave up daily prayer and reflection. Repletion sessions ought to be set up in such a way that they make room for relaxed reflection, for the airing of guilt feelings, cultural pressures and unrealistic expectations, for shared prayer, spiritual reading and meditation. The airing should take place in a gentle manner, wholly compassionate toward the pain of depletion without degenerating into mere "bitching sessions" where negativity and an atmosphere of murmuring abound.

Leaders of formative repletion sessions make clear to listeners that there are no "ten easy steps" to resolve spiritual depletion in the workplace. Dealing with deformation takes a lifetime, and then some. Pride resists fiercely the acceptance of limits. We all want to be perfect Christian professionals in a perfect society, but it exists nowhere on earth. Effectiveness is only possible if we remain receptive to the scant possibilities for improvement alive in every work situation without being discouraged by the limits we also behold. What we can do is to remain gently alert, vigilant, and quietly open to any signs of the onset of erosion. We try to catch ourselves and work this setback through before it reaches the stage of full-fledged depletion. Only then can we keep growing in our spiritual life in and through our work commitments.

We have to be in touch with loss of appreciation, empathy, joy; with an increase of irritability, resentment, griping. These negative attitudes make us and those around us more and more miserable. If we miss the early warning signals of erosion (indifference, inertia, withdrawal, cynicism), we are likely to be swept into the depletion of our spiritual life as laity. Even if this happens, we must remember that depletion is never final. In it resides the call for repletion in the Spirit. We may advance a few steps forward, but we are always in danger of falling behind. Therefore, in our weakness we shall always have to resource ourselves in the sustaining strength of the Spirit whose love is everlasting.

*Part Six*

*Commitment and Prayerful Living
as Laity*

# Chapter XXIII

# Daily Deepening and Spiritual Frigidity

Striving for a life of spiritual deepening in the midst of daily living means first of all that we must be willing to confront obstacles in the life of work and prayer that hinder or delay us on our journey to God. Likewise, in seeking a more harmonious presence to the Formation Mystery, we need to cultivate facilitating conditions that prompt further consonance. Let us exemplify this challenge by reflecting upon an oft overlooked obstacle that makes it difficult for us to integrate action and contemplation.

## *Spiritual Frigidity*

Spiritual frigidity is a type of impotence, religiously speaking. It connotes an inability to respond creatively to what God allows to occur in our lives. Spiritually frigid persons appear to lack the power or potency for surrender to the Mystery in a appreciatively abandoned manner. As a result, they do not experience the deeper transcendent meanings of daily occupations, family duties and fun times. They fall short in the realm of creativity and a generally hopeful outlook. Their lives tend to be somewhat flat and uninspiring. Religious devotions like meditation and spiritual reading, times of solitude and attendance at worship services are often experienced as tedious or painful to endure, as linked merely to obeying external rules.

Spiritual frigidity should not be confused with the "dark night of the soul," a fully graced experience understood as such by spiritual masters like St. John of the Cross. Frigidity, unlike clinging in deep faith to God even in midnight moments of not understanding, reveals itself when a person actually fears religious experiences of any kind or runs away from anything out of the immediate range of his or her control. This pre-focal fear has profound repercussions on one's prayer life, which is often marked by a lack of spontaneity and joy.

The same impotence mars one's ability to implement spirituality in a warm, intimate way in everyday life. As a result, frigid types may come across as cold, distant, withdrawn. One may interpret such postures as ascetic or pious but in reality they are based on fear of the transcendent.

The roots of this fear are frequently hidden from spiritually frigid persons. On the surface they may wish to be close to God and closer to other people. They may long for the peaceful conviction of God's fidelity to them. What they lack is the basic ingredient for such intimacy—the capacity to receive the peace that only God can give. This basic contentment is granted by surrender on our part to the Divine Will as ultimately gracious and benevolent.

In short, spiritually frigid people, not unlike those who suffer from this malady physically, are unable to surrender to anything that calls for risk and the relinquishing of control. Sadly, religious services, spiritual exercises and readings may hold no deeper meaning for them. They go through the motions of prayer but remain like prisoners surrounded by beautiful music, works of art and poetry, yet starving aesthetically.

## Need for Formation Counseling

Some may have to tackle this problem, depending on its severity, with a formation counselor who can help them to look at the underlying causes that have prevented them from enjoying a more relaxed and surrendered spiritual life. The help they receive may stimulate self-insight and quell the fears that suppressed the awareness of their transcendent calling in the first place. With God's grace, the well-prepared formation counselor can assist in releasing people of good will from the immobilizing grip of spiritual frigidity.

This obstacle can manifest itself in the form of complaining and grumbling about almost anything. These recurrent negative expressions represent the displacement of general spiritual dissatisfaction to another target, namely, numerous small annoyances most would be inclined to overlook as par-for-the-course in daily life. Instead they stir vast irritation.

It is the task of formation counselors to be patient with spiritually frigid clients when they are irritable, and understanding and accepting of them when they are importunate. Counselors should guard against the error of believing that either they themselves or the church is to blame for the symptom of spiritual frigidity and its concomitant fears, angers and annoyances. Such a misunderstanding might delay or even prevent insight into the real source of frigidity, which does not come from outside a person but from the inside.

## Influence of Childhood

Spiritual frigidity in committed Christians is usually rooted in an unconscious attitude of protest and resistance acquired in childhood and adolescence. This attitude may have been reinforced by a justified contemporary protest against various forms of religious imposition that were authoritarian, rigid, ladened with fear and guilt, and ultimately oppressive. Other distorted forms of piety may have been unrealistic, sentimental or secretly proud. Little wonder that certain people felt the need to protest against them. Trends in today's culture to exalt the rationalistic, legalistic, pragmatic, and technical management of life, oblivious of its mystery, are no help.

Formation counseling serves to undo the harm effected by personal and cultural obstacles to spiritual living. It fulfills this purpose by helping afflicted persons to achieve an in-depth understanding of religious frigidity and its sources. Once they understand the roots of this obstacle, people can begin to sense a change in their attitude and approach to life. This incipient transformation may be followed by a gradual reformation of the factors that contributed to the development of spiritual impotence in the first place.

People who suffer from the deficiency of frigidity cannot be held fully accountable for it. Their problem develops first in childhood and adolescence. It may also be partly a product of the influences of family, school, neighborhood, and church over which young people have no control. Neither were they in charge of their early emotional reactions against deformed religious practices and authority, which they justly or unjustly resented. However, now that some light has been shed on their problem, they can trace its unpleasant repercussions in both their professional and their familial life. From this moment on, spiritual frigidity, once an imprisoning obstacle, can be resolved and replaced by the free flow of their personality toward the transcendent. Their quest for spiritual maturity as committed Christians can once again be resumed.

## *Conditions for Overcoming Spiritual Frigidity*

Married or single persons must really sense and feel their own resistant emotions to anything associated with spirituality. They must allow depreciative fears and frigid responses to come to the surface of their consciousness. They may select for this disclosure a small but recurrent annoyance or some slightly self-destructive pattern of behavior, like pushing oneself unnecessarily beyond the boundaries of fatigue. The important thing is to dwell on this disposition or action, not to dismiss it, to let oneself feel the full measure of emotional energy behind it.

After some time one may begin to realize that there resides below the surface of what has been dismissed as a "bad habit," an apparently trifling matter, much more than meets the eye. One may discover beneath a commonplace complaint an all-pervasive resentment, a fear of failure, an inability to be intimate with anyone, God included. One may further discover the pent-up anger, the hostile, frightened feelings, lying just below the periphery of everyday depreciative attitudes.

During this process, one may move from annoyance to anger to hostile suspicion to sweeping put-downs of the church, society and authority in general. At a certain point we may be shocked by our own negativity. We may see at once that such defensiveness points to an underlying obstacle in which spiritual surrender, openness, and loving receptivity are virtually impossible for us to inaugurate and sustain.

The success of this process may only become apparent after a long period of time. Initially, spiritually frigid people may feel quite innocent of ever harboring hidden thoughts and emotions that are so intense and depreciative. Were the latter not present, they would not suffer from this kind of spiritual frigidity in the first place.

Many Christians have suppressed the intensity of their feelings, even from themselves, because they could not risk being overwhelmed by them. Therefore, they have learned over the years to conceal and contain them, even to redirect them toward picayune matters—anything to minimize them and, if possible, to deny their existence totally. However, only by allowing them to enter one's awareness as obstacles to prayer and presence can spiritually frigid people experience that the force of these feelings is not overwhelming. Apparently invincible obstacles can be rendered vincible. They discover to their surprise that these refused emotions will not destroy them. Once they taste a bit of freedom, even the most frigid of persons will gradually feel at home with the whole range of their emotions, and also their need to surrender to God.

## *Healing of Our Interiority*

Another reason why some people may be afraid to make this inward journey and to let their depreciative feelings come to the fore has to do with a secret fear that their ultimately irrational thoughts and feelings may have come to represent reality for them. Therefore, another condition for this healing to occur consists in a growing awareness that such deep and hidden fears about religion and spirituality are shaped early in life, primarily by one's relationships with parents and secondarily by contacts and encounters with teachers, ministers, priests, school companions and other peer groups.

These convictions about spirituality must be seen as basically irrational and unrealistic. One must come to understand them in great measure as defenses against one's own fixations and confusions in the realm of religion. They have no sufficient basis in fact; they do not pertain to real spirituality in the formative sense.

Sadly, religion and spirituality may have been communicated to us in a rigid or sentimental way. Consequently, we may have experienced any form of worship as that which keeps one infantile and wimpy, to say the least. Later in life, faced with a deeper transcendent commitment, we may have seemingly forgotten this fear. Still, the hidden anxiety will not go away, for it generates a subtle but steady resistance to surrender. Hence, it may become impossible, even for baptized Christians, to develop the receptive attitudes of prayerful persons, who live in spiritual abandonment.

With the help of grace, we may dare to allow these depreciative, frigid feelings and their underlying emotions to lessen in power over us so that we can at last be free to know and love God as we desire. As long as we do not explore antagonistic thoughts and feelings, any objective communication about spiritual abandonment will fall on deaf ears.

Still there is much hope for Christians who suffer from spiritual frigidity, especially for those who are willing to search courageously until they have exposed to the light every lingering antagonistic thought, emotion, or disposition that has poisoned their interiority until now. Once such obstacles become known, they can be subjected to appraisal and the test of reality. The spontaneous spiritual movement of the human personality toward the transcendent—blocked for years by the bane of religious frigidity—can be renewed.

Grace, which precedes and fosters the healing of our interiority, can now flow freely through a committed Christian ready to receive its transforming influence. Following this purification process one is obviously better prepared to comprehend and embrace a life of prayer and spiritual abandonment as essential steps along the way to Christian maturity.

## Chapter XXIV

# Spiritual Disciplines as Avenues to Committed Living

The longer we live, the more we sense our need for God's grace to sustain us in our quest to live as committed lay people. As avenues to maturity in faith, we may pursue in cooperation with grace certain disciplines that help us to meet God in everyday life. One fertile discipline is that of spiritual or formative reading.

Formative reading requires first of all that we become disciples of the word of God as it addresses us through the faith-filled words of scripture and the spiritual masters. This exercise of reading prepares us for committed Christian living. Important as reading for information is, it is insufficient for our purposes. If we read only to gather information, neglecting to deepen our interiority, we may actually widen rather than bridge the gap between us and God.

### *Spiritual Renewal*

In our attempts as laity to pay more attention to our spiritual lives, we need to maintain a balanced approach to the word "renewal." To preserve an appreciation for the spiritual classics, we must not focus so much on what is *new* that we forget to *re*-source ourselves in the texts, traditions, doctrines and directives of the church. Neither do we want to emphasize the resourcing phrase so much that we resist change and growth in relation to other people, to here and now situations, and to the world at large. New knowledge and its disclosure in texts can be seen as God's gift too. As readers, we share in the task of restoration while remaining open to the power of the Spirit to lead us where we never thought we would go.

Spiritual reading is at once a practice that returns us to the classics of our faith tradition while readying us for Christian service in a diversity of new and challenging situations. T. S. Eliot in his poem, "Choruses from 'The Rock,'" profiles our condition at this moment of history. He suggests in the opening lines that though ours is an age of technical progress, it may be, by the same token, an age of spiritual regression. He observes that we live in an endless cycle of idea and action, endless invention, endless experiment. Our age brings knowledge of motion, but not of stillness; knowledge of speech, but not of silence; knowledge of words and ignorance of the word, all our knowledge brings us nearer to our ignorance, all our ignorance brings us nearer to death, but nearness to death, no nearer to God. He asks starkly: Where is the life we have lost in living? Where is the wisdom we have lost in knowledge? Where is the knowledge we have lost in information? He then pronounces this sad judgment: The cycles of heaven in twenty centuries have brought us farther from God and nearer to the dust.

The poet's words touch us deeply. We too ask ourselves: Where is the life we have lost in living? Where is the wisdom we have lost in our efforts to gather information? Why do so many people choose death when God invites us to choose life, and life abundantly?

Perhaps the answers can only be forthcoming if we dare to look into our own interiority. Have we drunk so deeply of the gospel message that we are able to communicate it to others, if not by what we say or do, then by the way we are? Does our reading lead us to experience the liberation of the sons and daughters of God or have we lost our joy, our peace, our sense of serene service?

The art and discipline of reading the classics might have been alive and well in former times, but it has been somewhat neglected in our own. Why is this so? To respond to this question, we must contrast certain conditions emphasized in the past with certain obstacles we moderns face in our longing to relearn the art of spiritual reading.

## Attitudes Fostering Receptivity to God's Word

Why is this practice difficult for many? As a spiritual exercise, slowed down formative reading was meant to transform one's heart and mind, to stimulate meditation, to inspire action. A monk's day, for instance, was in great measure oriented around divine reading or *lectio divina*. To do it well, he developed special dispositions like "rumination." The word of God was like a precious morsel of food for the soul. One had to chew the text over and over again. In the process of digesting its wisdom, one hoped to grow in intimacy with God, uniting oneself slowly yet steadily with the Divine in the dark knowledge of faith.

Another attitude peculiar to the person engaged in formative reading is a change in one's conscious attention. One shifts from a "linear" to a "dwelling" mode of attentiveness. The word "dwelling"—and related words like abiding, resting, slowing down—signifies a kind of homecoming. The formative reader dwells upon, makes his or her home in, the words of holy scripture and the writings of the spiritual masters.

The attitude of dwelling fosters in turn that of docility or openness to the guidance of the Holy Spirit that may be granted through regular sessions of personal or shared spiritual reading. In a spirit of docility, the word is digested by the reader. One literally savors the wisdom that these words contain and listens with a special ear to their teaching. In this sense faith comes through hearing with an attentive ear, an ear attuned to the Spirit speaking to the heart of the reader through inspired authors and spiritual seekers whose texts are at once timely and of timeless value.

## *Cultural Obstacles to Formative Reading*

Contrast these attitudes of rumination, dwelling, and docility with what we see around us today. Rather than reading the classics, we fall victim to the compulsion to be current. We desire above all to be in-the-know. We feel deprived if we do not listen to the evening news or flip through the daily paper. There is nothing wrong with keeping up with the events of the world, but if we get caught in the compulsion to be current, we may be unable to stand still. We may forget to drink deeply from the well of words that speak perennially to the heart of the listener, that transcend the immediate demands of the everyday life run in the fast lane and that open one to lasting values.

What is the effect on our dwelling consciousness when day after day we are bombarded by radio, television, newspapers, billboards—a whole kaleidoscope of information that takes us outside of ourselves? This question is not meant to imply that we should never listen to the radio, read a newspaper, or watch television. It is simply to remind us that mere information gathering can be an obstacle to reading in depth. Do we spend too many hours in front of the television? Do we feel compelled to be current to the point of shelving scripture and the spiritual classics?

The attitude of rumination conflicts in particular with a

predominantly informational approach. Information, as opposed to rumination, has a tendency to fill us up, sometimes to the point of indigestion or information overload, whereas the reader of a deeper message feels like returning to it again and again. In formative reading there is always more to be said, whereas in informative reading we soon feel satiated.

The informational attitude, unlike that of docile rumination, seeks to conquer and master its subject matter. One takes in as much as one can hold, choosing quantity over quality. Similarly, one may indulge in a kind of "gourmet" spirituality. In this "taste test" approach, we may act as if spiritual reading were a great smorgasbord spread before us with little dumplings here, little canapes here, luscious cheeses in the corner. We go along and taste these treats, but seldom do we sit down and savor a good meal.

By the same token, there is a vast difference between "dwelling" reading and "linear" reading. Dwelling is a spiral movement. We move slowly from one sentence to another, resting in any one that appeals to our spirit and letting our mind and heart sink into it. Linear reading is horizontal, aimed at expanding our knowledge. While both styles are necessary, an exclusively linear approach may again cast one into a state of agitation, bent on always being "in" with the latest. This tendency admittedly markets best-sellers, but what does it do to scripture and the classics? It can be an obstacle to the life of the spirit in general by fostering in people a penchant for "pop" spirituality rather than maturation in faith.

What does outer informational listening do to the inner ear Jesus asks us to use, to the ear that is attentive not to what Dag Hammarskjold calls in *Markings* the "shouts and horns of the hunt" but to the silent whispers of the Holy Spirit? Are we not prone to escape the discipline of meditative reflection? Do we not delight in the art of labeling a book "conservative" or "progressive" and dismissing it accordingly. Once a label is applied, we can escape the sometimes painful moment of reflection when we have to dwell on what the text is saying to us about our faith.

The outer information-gathering ear is especially tempted to dismiss as irrelevant ancient texts, for after all "what can a relic of the past teach us today?" This shallow response overlooks the lasting wisdom found in scripture and the literature of spirituality. It cuts us off from a significant source of adult Christian formation.

## *Restoration of Reading*

To restore the art of spiritual reading, we have to try once again, in our own way, to devote time to this exercise, even if we do it only for ten or fifteen minutes a day. We can sit down and read a favorite psalm, not mechanically but with a heart set to savor its meaning. Instead of turning from page to page searching for something new, we may stay with one phrase or even one line. Perhaps through this slowed down approach, we may meet God in the sacrament of the present moment.

Faithful living implies, therefore, setting aside time for spiritual reading. Even though our age tends to draw us away from interiority, preventing rather than encouraging us to ruminate, dwell and listen with the inner ear, we must return to scripture and the classics if we want our spiritual life to grow.

Typical of the contemporary western mind is the penchant to gather information, to label, to categorize, and to spin abstractions instead of simply being with the message in a reflective state of wonder, awe and adoration. It is in this state of dwelling presence that the words of holy scripture, as well as those of classic and contemporary spiritual masters, come alive for us. Recall Psalm 139, which suggests that even before a word is on our tongue, behold, the Lord knows the whole of it. Behind us and before, he hems us in and rests his hand upon us. Such knowledge is too wonderful for us to imagine, too lofty for us to attain. The psalmist assures us that the Lord knows what is in our hearts even before we speak. He invites us to enter into the dark knowledge of faith beyond the input that comes to us through our argumentative intellects alone. Over and above our development as scientific analyzers, we are called to be receptively present to the Lord in faith, hope and love.

One could compare reading a spiritual text in this fashion to puzzling a "koan." A "koan" is a riddle that a Buddhist spiritual master might give to a disciple, not because he wants the disciple to solve the puzzle logically but because he wants him to live in the wonderment of not being able to come up with a logical solution. If the disciple were to decipher the message, he would become a mere master of the word, perhaps taking pride in his expertise and thus losing the whole point of the exercise—to foster humility and learn that the gift of enlightenment is beyond one's power to control.

The western disciple, in a similar vein, might desire, when reading a text from scripture, to become, for example, a master of exegesis, linguistics, or biblical history only. This mastery, however necessary for other purposes and useful as a remote preparation for spiritual reading, could be an obstacle to formative reading itself if the reader persists in only exercising his or her capacity to master the text by means of study. Analyzing the text is one thing. Imbibing it spiritually in intimate presence to God is another.

The "koan" in eastern spirituality is thus a paradoxical problem with no logical solution. It is to be kept before the mind of the disciple day and night. Eventually it will be the means by which he will pierce through the knowledge gained by the logical intellect to another level of reason where one is open to the Mystery. An exemplary "koan" might be, "What was the shape of your original face before you were born?"

Another: "You known the sound of two hands clapping; what is the sound of one hand clapping?"

A clever westerner who hears this "koan" might try to solve it literally by clapping one hand. The guru would surely smack him on the shoulders as a friendly sign that he was missing the point. He was trying to solve the problem, whereas the purpose of the "koan" is to let the disciple live in the realm of paradox that generates mental anguish. He is reminded, then, of his incapacity to resolve the great mysteries of humanity's relationship with the Divine. Mere logical intelligence cannot break through to the kind of knowledge that lifts reason into the realm of faith.

A monk once asked his guru, "Who is the Buddha?" The disciple held his breath in anticipation of a profound answer that would clarify the intricate theology of eastern mysticism. The master paused and then said to him, "Who is the Buddha? Three yards of flax," and suddenly he was illuminated. The wise master did not answer his question in a technical way; he chose instead to baffle technical intelligence so he could help the seeker reach a level of wisdom that lifted him beyond what his faithless mind could grasp.

The discursive aspect of the intellect, so highly developed in the west, facilitates logical reasoning and information sciences, but in and by itself it cannot grasp the full significance of spiritual texts as life messages. The text is an appeal, not an answer; a question, not a solution. Formative reading invites the reader to flow with experience and enlightened insight enmeshed in the text, to re-experience it, to make it one's own.

## *Reading and Meditation*

Ordinarily in our busy, active work days, we live on the level of discursive reasoning. We have to manage our lives, organize schedules, get things done, conduct meetings—all extremely important tasks for which we need a discursive, managing intellect. However, we have to be able, on a regular basis, to "bracket" this functional mind when we approach a spiritual text in faith. We must now go to the text not so much to master it as to humbly dispose ourselves to be mastered by it, by its power to penetrate the surface and plunge us into a deeper level of reason. What awakens then are not merely our exterior senses but those more interior intuitions that ready us for the experience of divine intimacy, should God grant it to us.

Beyond the information that comes through the discursive intellect, we discover in an experiential way what it is like to live in the awareness of God's presence that transcends explanatory effort. We attain that knowledge of the heart spoken of in the writings of mystics like Teresa of Avila and John of the Cross. Both writers remain submissive to the teaching church, to its fundamental doctrines and traditions. They are utterly immersed in the words of holy scripture. And yet, in their writing, they do not seek so much to explain these mysteries of faith as to show us how to live them.

Whereas theology helps us understand the truth of revelation, spirituality points to their proximate lived reality. Formative spirituality asks not so much *why* we live the faith but *how* we live it. This knowledge of the heart is what classical spiritual masters want to communicate so that we, their readers, can come to a more personal living of the mystery and majesty of our faith.

If we wish to hear the Spirit speaking to us through the words of the masters, we have to be at peace with the fact that their message may at times be purposefully cryptic. We may not understand it on first reading and, in a sense, it should not be understood that easily. New layers of meaning continue to be revealed to us each time we return to the text. As we develop and deepen, as we open ourselves more and more to

God's grace alive and at work in us, the words we read may be the same, but their meaning is different. In a sense, the text discloses its secrets to us as we grow in wisdom and grace before the Lord.

Texts that seemed easy to understand at first may become more paradoxical. The faith we took for granted challenges us anew. God becomes a "dazzling darkness," but how can the darkness be dazzling? The Spirit is a "speaking silence," but how can silence speak? What does it really mean to lose myself in order to find my true self in God, or to decrease that God may increase? How mysterious, strange and wonderful is this dark knowledge of faith! God, the almighty, transcendent One, becomes a little child in Bethlehem, dies and rises, calls us by name, commissions us to go forth and teach all nations.

Wonder enables us to contemplate, as from a divine viewpoint, the unity of all created reality in Christ. This seeing in faith is a never-ending process, leading to the beatific vision. To say, "Lord, I am not worthy to receive you, only say the word and I shall be healed," is to participate in an intimate moment of divine communion during which the word blesses our brokenness and makes us whole. And are we not a people in need of healing today? Are we not a people who more than ever have to surrender ourselves to the healing power of the word, a word given to us every day in scripture, liturgy, and our spiritual reading, provided we dispose ourselves to its reception through proper attitudes of listening.

### *Attitudes That Ready Us for a Wider Vision*

To ready ourselves for healing, we must remain humble. Teresa of Avila calls humility the queen of the virtues. It is a first condition for listening with the inner ear. "Open wide your mouth, and I will fill it," we read in Psalm 81. It is as if God reminds us in no uncertain terms: "Do all that you can to listen to me, but know, in the long run, in the last analysis, it is not you who do it, but I—I working and living in you." In other words, our task is to become not masters but servants of the word. Mastery is appropriate when we are composing a term paper or taking minutes at a meeting. But when we turn to sacred writers, our role is different. In docility to the Spirit, who leads us to all truth and who searches the deep things of God, we are to use our times of spiritual reading to deepen our knowledge and love of God and to reaffirm the gift of our faith.

Spiritual reading begins with holy scripture; it then moves to the masters of pre-reformation spirituality: Augustine, Bernard of Clairvaux, Thomas à Kempis, Julian of Norwich, Teresa of Avila, John of the Cross, to mention only a few. Of great importance, too, are masters of reformation spirituality, such as John Donne, George Fox, John Wesley, Søren Kierkegaard, C. S. Lewis, and Dietrich Bonhoeffer. The collection of classics carries us into our times, with such contemporary masters of spirituality as T. S. Eliot, Edith Stein, and Thomas Merton. These writers share insights on many facets of the spiritual life. The path along which they lead us is not always smooth; it often bears the sign of the cross. It is a path along which one freely chooses to follow One who by worldly standards was a failure. Yet he asks his disciples to trust that his words are true and that his kingdom is not of this world. In the background of all that we see, there is another reality to which we are drawn, an eternal depth that embraces every passing epiphany.

Humility, docility, receptivity—such attitudes ready us to participate in this vision, while simplicity enables us to set proper priorities to execute it. One way of simplifying may be to choose, in addition to holy scripture, one or two spiritual writers who really speak to us. If we feel we have to read a whole pile of books, we may get discouraged before we start. We may never begin to read a little because we are so busy worrying about reading a lot. The important thing is to choose one or two texts that enable us to begin the process of regular reading of the classics. It is not necessary to read everything. It is wiser to select a few texts and really enter into them than to want to read many—a goal that may never materialize. We will discover, if the writers chosen are sufficiently deep, that fundamental themes and dynamics of the spiritual life repeat themselves century after century. It is as if each age has to discover again what has already been disclosed by a previous generation.

For example, in a world full of noise, we are more than ever in need of people who witness for the value of silence and slowed down reading. It is good even in a functional setting to maintain some aspects of a vacation mood. Remember what happens when we go to the seashore for a week or so. We probably say, "Thank God! I don't even want to read a newspaper. It's wonderful to be out of the working world for a while." When we re-enter it, it feels as if we have been watching a soap opera. The storyline picks up where it left off when we departed. Our intention is not to mitigate the importance of being current. It is only to say that maintaining a vacation mood helps when we do spiritual reading.

We also have to keep in mind the real meaning of the life call of laity. If it implies witnessing to the basic truths of spiritual awakening and deepening, then it may not be absolutely necessary for us to be always media-oriented. It is exactly in ceasing to be current, in maintaining a vacation mood, that we may hear once again the secret whisperings of the Spirit to live a committed Christian life. Then we may be able to communicate by our life what we have heard of God to others; then our very existence may become an embodiment of Jesus' infinite love for humanity.

How simple life would be were we able to orient everything we say or do or think around these themes of committed living so well articulated in the spiritual classics: to wholly trust in the Lord, to serve God in purity of heart and poverty of spirit, to remain simple in a complex world.

Reading the classics enables us to withdraw periodically to gain perspective. To read formatively is to retire momentarily from our busy life of service so that we can once again re-source ourselves in the wisdom of the masters. Only then can we appraise whether the Spirit is truly speaking in our life or whether we are merely listening to our own voices. The words of the masters greatly aid us in this assessemnt. As the complexities of modern life compound, we need more than ever to read the classics. Their appeal for simplicity becomes all the more compelling in a world where, as Henry David Thoreau said in *Walden*, "The mass of men lead lives of quiet desperation."

Committed Christians are called to be shepherds of the sacred dimension of reality, to transform the world into the house of God. There is an acute need in our culture for lay people committed to the message of the classics. To read these books devoutly is to be led out of the wasteland of spiritual regression toward the promised land of Christian maturity. They teach us first-hand that heaven and earth may pass away but the words of the Lord stand fast forever.

# Chapter XXV

# Prayer Life of the Laity

In moments of prayer and committed service, we are clothed in Christ's love. He wants this love to radiate out through us toward the weak, the temperamental, sick and poor. He wants this love to permeate our own confused and suffering lives. Those who seem fools and failures, those who cross us, who hold different values, who threaten us by alien attitudes, are no less worthy recipients of our prayer and service.

The gift of divine transforming love is waiting for us. It surrounds our heart on all sides. Standing at the door, God knocks incessantly to enter. Our opening of that door is prayer.

### *The Path of Prayer*

We can only learn to pray by praying. We should not restrict ourselves to reading books about prayer, no more than lovers should be satisfied with reading books about love. We may get so wrapped up in words about how to pray that we forget to pray. Without the practice of prayer, words about it do not mean much. Moreover, not everything about prayer can be put into words. Even the words of the scriptures about prayer will only mean something when we try to live and experience them.

## Different Ways of Prayer

There are many ways in which we can learn to pray. Each way is limited. We may learn from all of them. The only important thing is that we follow the way the Spirit leads us. Some would say that to pray is to learn to talk to God. The advice is true, but it does not go far enough. It may leave us with the impression that God is a distant person. We have to learn also that God is near to us, truly within us.

Others teach prayer as a conversation. This counsel is nearer to the truth. The difficulty is that we cannot hear God as we can hear the voice of a friend, parent, child, or spouse. It takes time to learn how to hear a Silent Voice in the intimacy of our heart.

To learn to pray, others suggest, we must learn to think about Christ, the saints, the mysteries of our faith, the texts of scripture. This guidance makes sense too. We think about ourselves and others and what happens around us. Why not choose to think also about God and God's words? This kind of prayer is meditation. It is not difficult to learn. It comes naturally to us, for we all meditate, though not always on our faith. We may meditate on the person we love, on the illness or death of a friend, on a novel we have read, on a spectator sport we witnessed.

Meditation becomes prayerful when it focuses on the knowledge and love of God. Learning this kind of prayer helps us to gain interest in God and in the Bible. Still we may see God as outside ourselves. We may get caught in mental games rather than learning to love and admire the Spirit.

Some tell us that the way they learned to pray was by reflection on their life. Involved as we are in our meetings and occupations, we spontaneously feel the need to muse about what happens to us, how we handled a situation, how it affected us and others. We can learn to do this prayerfully by bringing God into our reflections. We sit down quietly, and while the events of the day flow through our mind, we keep our hearts turned to the Holy.

Others advise us to develop a personal relationship with God. They compare this way of learning with the growth of a human relationship. It keeps growing through talking and being with each other. Finally, there may slowly emerge something we cannot describe in words but which reveals itself as true, lasting love. We have simply fallen in love with God. As this love grows deeper, we need less and less words. We can be silent together and enjoy being close.

Learning to pray this way can be aided by imagining ourselves in a relation of friendship with Jesus and his mother as we know them from the gospels. This way of prayer is excellent as long as it satisfies us. In the long run it may have its drawbacks too. God may call us gradually to a less tangible, more spiritual prayer. It would then be an obstacle on the path were we to cling to our former, more imaginative way of praying. It proved helpful in the beginning, but now we must let it go.

## *Prayer of Presence*

A deeper way of learning to pray is to try to live in the presence of God. This is the beginning of always praying as the gospel writers and St. Paul in his epistles recommend. We try in a relaxed way to become aware of the Divine Presence during our waking hours. We need the grace of quiet concentration and perseverance to develop this disposition. Gradually, awareness of God's presence becomes an underlying theme of our life, an undercurrent of our stream of consciousness that never leaves us totally. This silent orientation is more spiritual and less bound to images than former kinds of prayer.

It is a matter of heeding the psalmist's directive: "Be still and know that I am God" (Ps. 46:10).

Learning to know God this way in prayer cannot be reduced to the everyday way in which we know people and events. It implies making room in our heart for an experience of God's loving presence deep within us and around us.

Learning to pray is as basic to our spiritual life as learning to breathe is for a newborn infant. Learning to pray will not always be easy. God allows periods of aridity in which praying seems empty and dull. But our Father in heaven also grants periods of peace and love, indescribable in their beauty.

To learn to pray, we must try in inner quiet to grow in living faith, in the conviction that God is alive and at work deep within us. We must be ready to give some time and effort to daily prayer, to bear with boredom until in God's own time we are awakened to that for which our soul longs.

## *Practicing Prayer*

Remaining in God's presence is the condition of always praying. There must be a way of keeping in touch with God that is open to each of us. How do we keep in touch with our family, our best friends, our beloved? We do so in many ways, through visits, postcards, letters, telephone calls, conversations, dinners. It is necessary that we do these things to keep our relationships alive.

Remaining in God's presence happens in a similar way. Jesus himself gave the example. The core of his life was keeping in touch with the Father. Time and again he created moments of stillness in his life to be alone with God. These moments flowed over into the rest of his earthly existence.

Jesus was always abiding with his Father. This presence was nourished by the words of the Hebrew scriptures on which he had meditated since his youth.

To follow Jesus' life of prayer is to create, as he did, moments of stillness in our lives. It is to pay attention to God's words as they come to us in our reading of the scriptures or in the liturgy. As soon as a word strikes us as personally meaningful or fills us with peace, we should treasure it in our hearts. We should take it with us in our daily life and return to it again and again. It is our point of contact with the Lord who remains in us; it is our way of remaining in him.

We may collect words and sentences that have proven to be of help to us in this regard. They can serve as bridges between our busy day and the Lord within us. There are many unscheduled moments during the day—waiting at a stop sign or traffic light, standing in line at a checkout counter, sitting in a doctor's waiting room, walking from classroom to office, doing the dishes or making beds. We should welcome such occasions as opportunities to dwell on the words we have chosen as evocative of our presence to God, of God's presence to us. We do not reason about such words; rather we allow them gently to penetrate our hearts and minds as fragrant oil saturates a sponge. Neither should we be forceful in our attentiveness. Ours should be a stance of waiting in patience, ready to receive the imprint of the word in the depth of our soul, yet also ready to bear with the absence of any consolation.

What counts is steadily returning to the words of the Lord, of disciples, saints and spiritual writers. This return will keep our life oriented toward our deeper calling and commitment. We shall then truly abide in God. Even if we do not feel the effects of this dwelling, we can be sure that in time God will grant us momentary illuminations, brief glimpses, passing but real experiences of a Presence beyond words. Our awe may be fleeting but its impact is lasting. In the end we may receive the grace of praying always. We may have found the key to commitment, the key to Christian maturity.

# Bibliography

à Kempis, Thomas. *The Imitation of Christ.* Trans. Harold C. Gardiner. Garden City, N.Y.: Image Books, 1955.

Aelred of Rievaulx. *Spiritual Friendship.* Kalamazoo, Mich.: Cistercian Publications, 1977.

Bartley, William Warren. *The Retreat to Commitment.* New York: Knopf, 1962.

Bellah, Robert N. *Habits of the Heart: Individualism and Commitment in American Life.* Berkeley, Calif.: University of California Press, 1985.

Blauner, Robert. *Alienation and Freedom: The Factory Worker and His Industry.* Chicago: University of Chicago Press, 1964.

Bloom, Alan. *The Closing of the American Mind.* New York: Simon and Schuster, 1987.

Bonhoeffer, Dietrich. *Meditating on the Word.* Trans., ed., David McI. Gracie. Cambridge, Mass.: Cowley Publications, 1986.

Burke, John G., ed. *The New Technology and Human Values.* Belmont, Calif.: Wadsworth Publications, 1966.

Carretto, Carlo. *I, Francis.* Maryknoll, N.Y.: Orbis Books, 1982.

Ciszek, Walter J. *He Leadeth Me.* Garden City, N.Y.: Image Books, Doubleday, 1975.

Clemmons, William P. *Discovering the Depths: Guidance in Personal Growth.* Nashville, Tenn.: Broadman Press, 1987.

Cummings, Charles. *The Mystery of the Ordinary.* San Francisco: Harper and Row, 1982.

de Caussade, Jean Pierre. *Abandonment to Divine Providence.* Trans. John Beevers. Garden City, N.Y.: Image Books, Doubleday, 1975.

de Vinek, Jose. *Revelations of Women Mystics: From Middle Ages to Modern Times.* New York: Alba House, 1985.

Doohan, Leonard. *The Laity: A Bibliography.* Wilmington, Del.: Michael Glazier, 1987.

Dostoevsky, F. *The Idiot* New York: Bantam Books, 1971.

Droel, William L. and Gregory F. Augustine Pierce. *Confident and Competent: A Challenge for the Lay Church.* Notre Dame, Ind.: Ave Maria Press, 1976.

Edelwich, Jerry with Archie Brodsky. *Burn-Out: Stages of Disillusionment in the Helping Professions.* New York: Human Sciences Press, 1980.

Eliot, T.S. *The Waste Land and Other Poems.* New York: Harcourt Brace and World, 1934.

English, John. *Choosing Life.* New York: Paulist Press, 1978.

Fittipaldi, Silvio. *How To Pray Always without Always Praying.* Notre Dame, Ind.: Fides/Claretian, 1978.

Foster, Richard J. *Celebration of Discipline: The Path to Spiritual Growth.* New York: Harper and Row, 1978.

Fowler, James W. *Stages of Faith: The Psychology of Human Development and the Quest for Meaning.* San Francisco: Harper and Row, 1981.

*Francis and Clare: The Complete Works.* Classics of Western Spirituality. New York: Paulist Press, 1982.

Frank, Anne. *Diary of a Young Girl.* Trans. B.M. Mooyaart-Doubleday. New York: Modern Library, 1952.

Freudenberger, H. J. *The Ego and the Id.* New York: Bantam Books, 1980.

Gratton, Carolyn. *Guidelines for Spiritual Direction.* Denville, N.J.: Dimension Books, 1980.

Groothuis, Douglas R. *Unmasking the New Age*. Downers Grove, Ill.: InterVarsity Press, 1986.

Grou, Jean-Nicholas. *How To Pray*. Rpt., London: James Clarke, 1964.

Guardini, Romano. *Freedom, Grace and Destiny: Three Chapters on the Interpretation of Existence*. New York: Pantheon, 1961.

Guelluy, Robert. *Christian Commitment to God and to the World*. Rome: Desclèe, 1965.

Guigo II. *The Ladder of Monks and Twelve Meditations*. Garden City, N.Y.: Image Books, Doubleday, 1978.

Hammarskjöld, Dag. *Markings*. Trans. W.H. Auden and Leif Sjöberg. London: Faber and Faber, 1964.

Heider, John. *The Tao of Leadership: Lao Tzu's Tao Te Adapted for a New Age*. Atlanta: Humanics New Age, 1985.

Herbstrith, Waltraud. *Edith Stein: A Biography*. San Francisco: Harper and Row, 1971.

Jessey, Cornelia. *The Prayer of Cosa: Praying in the Way of St. Francis of Assisi*. Minneapolis, Minn.: Winston Press, 1985.

*John and Charles Wesley: Selected Writings and Hymns*. Classics of Western Spirituality. New York: Paulist Press, 1981.

Jones, Alan. *Exploring Spiritual Direction: An Essay on Christian Friendship*. Minneapolis, Minn.: Winston Press, 1982.

*Julian of Norwich: Showings*. Classics of Western Spirituality. New York: Paulist Press, 1978.

Kavanaugh, Kieran and Otilio Rodriguez, trans. *The Collected Works of St. John of the Cross*. Washington, D.C.: Institute of Carmelite Studies, 1979.

———. *The Collected Works of St. Teresa of Avila*. Vol. One. Washington, D.C.: Institute of Carmelite Studies, 1976.

———. *The Collected Works of St. Teresa of Avila. Vol. Two.* Washington, D.C.: Institute of Carmelite Studies, 1980.

Kelly, Bernard J. *Lay Spirituality: Its Theory and Practice.* London: Sheed and Ward, 1980.

Keniston, Kenneth. *The Uncommitted: Alienated Youth in American Society.* New York: Harcourt, Brace and World, 1965.

Kierkegaard, Søren. *Purity of Heart Is To Will One Thing.* New York: Harper Torchbooks, 1956.

Kiesler, Charles A. *The Psychology of Commitment.* New York: Academic Press, 1971.

Knight, David. *His Word: Letting It Take Root—and Bear Fruit—in Our Lives.* Cincinnati: St. Anthony Messenger Press, 1970.

Kohlberg, Lawrence. *Essays on Moral Development.* Volume One. *The Philosophy of Moral Development.* San Francisco: Harper and Row, 1981.

Leckey, Dolores R. *Laity Stirring the Church: Prophetic Questions.* Philadelphia: Fortress Books, 1987.

———. *The Ordinary Way: A Family Spirituality.* New York: Crossroad, 1982.

———. *Practical Spirituality for Lay People.* Kansas City: Sheed and Ward, 1987.

Levinson, D.J. *The Seasons of a Man's Life.* New York: Ballantine Books, 1978.

Lewis, C.S. *Mere Christianity.* New York: Macmillan, 1960.

Lindbergh, A.M. *Gift from the Sea.* New York: Random House, 1955.

Marcel, Gabriel. *Creative Fidelity.* New York: Farrar, Straus, 1964.

Maslow, Abraham H. *Motivation and Personality.* New York: Harper and Row, 1970.

May, Gerald C. *Care of Mind, Care of Spirit: Psychiatric Dimensions of Spiritual Direction.* San Francisco: Harper and Row, 1982.

May, R. *Love and Will*. New York: W.W. Norton, 1969.

Mayeroff, M. *On Caring*. New York: Harper and Row, 1971.

McNeill, Donald P., Douglas A. Morrison and Henri J.M. Nouwen. *Compassion: A Reflection on the Christian Life*. Garden City, N.Y.: Doubleday, 1966.

Mead, Margaret. *Culture and Commitment: A Study of the Generation Gap*. New York: Doubleday, 1970.

Merton, Thomas. *Sign of Jonas*. New York: Image Books, Doubleday, 1956.

Muto, Susan. *Blessings That Make Us Be: A Formative Approach to Living the Beatitudes*. New York: Crossroad, 1984.

―――. *Celebrating the Single Life: A Spirituality for Single Persons in Today's World*. Garden City, N.Y.: Image Books, Doubleday, 1985.

―――. *Pathways of Spiritual Living*. New York: Doubleday, 1984. Rpt., Petersham, Mass.: St. Bede's, 1988.

―――. *A Practical Guide to Spiritual Reading*. Denville, N.J.: Dimension Books, 1976.

―――. *Renewed at Each Awakening: The Formative Power of Sacred Words*. Denville, N.J.: Dimension Books, 1979.

Nouwen, Henri J.M. *Reaching Out: The Three Movements of the Spiritual Life*. Garden City, N.Y.: Doubleday, 1966.

―――. *The Wounded Healer: Ministry in Contemporary Society*. Garden City, N.Y.: Doubleday, 1972.

Oates, Wayne E. *Confessions of a Workaholic*. New York: Abingdon Press, 1971.

Puls, Joan. *Every Bush Is Burning*. Foreword by Dr. Susan Muto. Mystic, Conn.: Twenty-Third Publications, 1985.

―――. *A Spirituality of Compassion*. Mystic, Conn.: Twenty-Third Publications, 1988.

*Quaker Spirituality: Selected Writings.* Classics of Western Spirituality. New York: Paulist Press, 1984.

Rahner, Karl. *The Christian Commitment.* New York: Sheed and Ward, 1963.

Rees, Daniel, et al. *Consider Your Call: A Theology of Monastic Life Today.* Kalamazoo, Mich.: Cistercian Publications, 1978.

Rosewell, Pamela. *Five Silent Years of Corrie ten Boom.* Grand Rapids, Mich.: Zondervan Books, 1986.

Ryan, John K., trans. *The Confessions of St. Augustine.* Garden City, N.Y.: Image Books, Doubleday, 1960.

Siegal, Bernie S. *Love, Medicine and Miracles: Lessons Learned about Self-Healing from a Surgeon's Experience with Exceptional Patients.* New York: Harper and Row, 1986.

Steere, Douglas V. *Together in Solitude.* New York: Crossroad, 1985.

Storms, Sister Kathleen. *Simplicity of Life as Lived in the Everyday.* Washington, D.C.: University Press of America, 1983.

ten Boom, Corrie. *The Hiding Place.* Great Britain: Hodder and Stoughton, 1971.

Terkel, Studs. *Working: People Talk about What They Do All Day and How They Feel about What They Do.* New York: Ballantine Books, 1972.

Thoreau, Henry David. *Walden.* New York: Bramhall House, 1961.

Tillich, P. *The Courage To Be.* New Haven, Conn.: Yale University Press, 1963.

Toffler, Alvin. *Future Shock.* New York: Random House, 1970.

Van Dusen, Henry P. *Dag Hammarskjöld: The Man and His Faith.* New York: Harper, 1964.

van Kaam, Adrian. *The Dynamics of Spiritual Self Direction.* Denville, N.J.: Dimension Books, 1976.

———. *Looking for Jesus*. Denville, N.J.: Dimension Books, 1978.

———. *On Being Involved*. Denville, N.J.: Dimension Books, 1969.

———. *The Roots of Christian Joy*. Denville, N.J.: Dimension Books, 1985.

———. *The Science of Formative Spirituality: Fundamental Formation*, Volume I. New York: Crossroad/Continuum, 1983.

———. *The Science of Formative Spirituality: Human Formation*, Volume II. New York: Crossroad/Continuum, 1985.

———. *The Science of Formative Spirituality: Formation of the Human Heart*, Volume III. New York: Crossroad/Continuum, 1986.

———. *The Science of Formative Spirituality: Scientific Formation*, Volume IV. New York: Crossroad/Continuum, 1987.

———. *In Search of Spiritual Identity*. Denville, N.J.: Dimension Books, 1975.

———. *The Transcendent Self: Formative Spirituality of the Middle, Early and Late Years of Life*. Denville, N.J.: Dimension Books, 1979.

———. *The Vowed Life*. Denville, N.J.: Dimension Books, 1968.

———and Susan Muto. *Am I Living a Spiritual Life?* Denville, N.J.: Dimension Books, 1978.

———and Susan Muto. *Practicing the Prayer of Presence*. Denville, N.J.: Dimension Books, 1980.

Von Durckheim, K. *Daily Life as Spiritual Exercise*. San Francisco: Harper and Row, 1972.

Wells, Ronald V. *Spiritual Disciplines for Everyday Living*. Schenectady, N.Y.: Character Resource Press, 1982.

Whitehead, Evelyn E. and James D. Whitehead. *Christian Life Patterns: The Psychological Challenge and Religious Invitation of Adult Life*. Garden City, N.Y.: Image Books, Doubleday, 1982.